week*LIGHT*

super-fast meals to make you feel good

photography by con poulos

WEEKLIGHT
Copyright © Donna Hay Pty Ltd 2019
Design copyright © Donna Hay Pty Ltd 2019
Photography copyright © Con Poulos 2019
Recipes and styling: Donna Hay
Art direction and design: Chi Lam
Copy editor: Abby Pfahl
Senior designer: Hannah Schubert
Recipe testing: Tessa Immens, Madeleine Jeffreys, Samantha Coutts
Merchandising: Alex Zehntner, Andreas Zehntner
dh Brand and business manager: Virginia Ford
dh Sponsorship and collaborations manager: Ruby Gillard
dh Chief financial officer: Karen Hay

Fourth Estate
An imprint of HarperCollins*Publishers*

First published in Australia and New Zealand in 2019
by HarperCollins*Publishers* Australia Pty Limited
ABN 36 009 913 517 harpercollins.com.au

HarperCollins*Publishers*
Level 13, 201 Elizabeth Street, Sydney NSW 2000
Unit D1, 63 Apollo Drive, Rosedale, Auckland 0632, New Zealand
A 53, Sector 57, Noida, UP, India
1 London Bridge Street, London SE1 9GF, United Kingdom
Bay Adelaide Centre, East Tower, 22 Adelaide Street West, 41st floor, Toronto, Ontario M5H 4E3, Canada
195 Broadway, New York NY 10007, USA

A catalogue record for this book is available from the National Library of Australia
ISBN: 978 1 4607 5811 3

On the cover: edamame avo smash super-green fritters, page 160

Reproduction by Splitting Image
Printed and bound in China by RR Donnelley on 140gsm Lucky Bird Uncoated Woodfree
6 5 4 3 2 1 19 20 21 22

donna hay

weeklight

super-fast meals to make you feel good

FOURTH ESTATE

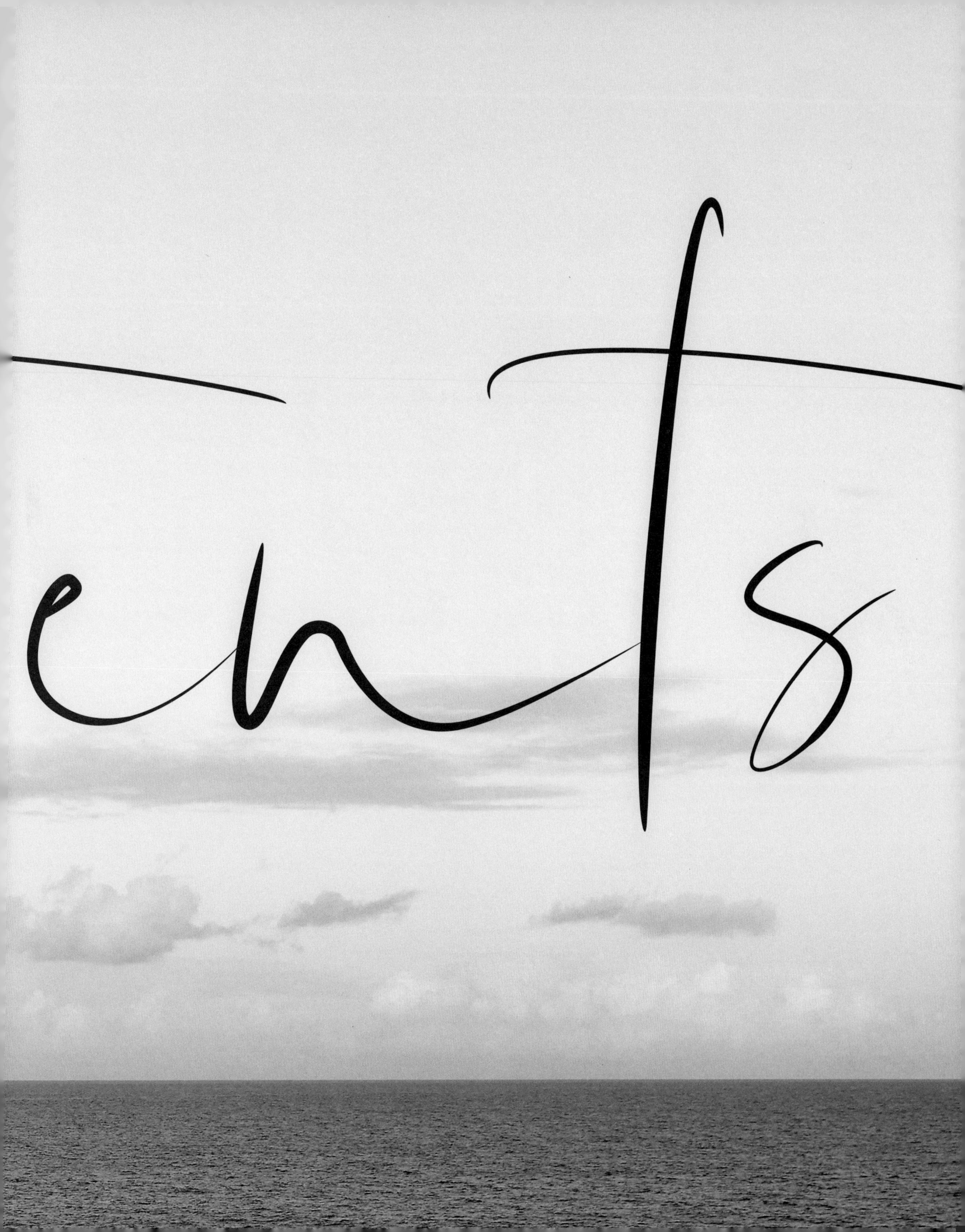

’ve always loved the way real food makes ME FEEL, but I think it’s time to revamp the way we *prepare it*. Let’s begin by REINVENTING some of the vegetables we know so well, let’s take a look at them with *fresh eyes*. In this book, cabbage becomes a *caramelised* CRISPY PANCAKE. Pure and clean greens, like silverbeet and spinach, SPRING TO LIFE in nourishing bowls with grains and *creamy dressings*. No longer the side dishes, the back-up dancers, *the understudies*, vegetables here have EARNED THEIR PLACE to be *front and centre* on your plate. So you’ll eat them not just to refuel and *re-energise*, but to indulge in all of the FLAVOUR.

how
to
be
healthier

be adventurous

Making sure your body gets all the nutrients it needs can be as straightforward as choosing a wide variety of foods. I hear lots about eating the colours of the rainbow – such a simple thing to keep in mind while you're shopping. It's easy to fall into the trap of buying the same fruit and veg week-in, week-out. But exploring ingredients and recipes outside our comfort zone can be a form of adventure – you can cook broccoli on the barbecue or blitz it and make a pizza base; you can caramelise nutrient-rich Brussels sprouts, cover them in creamy tahini lemon dressing and top with honeyed walnuts – yum! In these pages you'll find so many fresh ideas that will inspire you to expand your vegetable choices, as well as lots of new ways with your old faves.

be organised

I get it – cooking healthy meals takes a bit of planning and shopping (albeit for beautiful fresh ingredients). I don't always get the juggle right, but with a few practical steps it can feel a whole lot more achievable. Preparation is the key – and more veg naturally means more prep, but there are some sneaky shortcuts! Invest in a few handy tools and it becomes a breeze. My top three? A good-quality julienne peeler for shredding carrots and zucchinis, a mandolin for sharp, zero-fuss slicing and a food processor to chop cauliflower or broccoli in a flash. Once you're cooking, think ahead a little and make extra of some things to save time – like a big batch of brown rice, freekeh or quinoa – then freeze what's left into individual portions. Same goes for pasta sauce, fritters and soups.

be realistic

Life is fun, but it's full! I'm a big believer that eating is meant to be a pleasure and turning your whole dining routine upside-down in one hit is not fun, for anyone. Instead, try to integrate one small step at a time, one meat-free dinner a week or one new recipe that will push the boundaries. Be realistic and do what works for you. I know that I struggle to get the shopping done in normal store hours, but I've found a great online fruit and vegetable delivery service. Then when I'm at my local markets on the weekend, I'll chat to my friends at the organic stall to get a feel for what's in season (or just delicious right now!). Second to that, follow your greengrocer on social media. It's a whole new world of tips and information.

modern

makeover

*T*here's a lot to be said for those SIMPLE FAMILY MEALS we cook *all the time*, like spaghetti bolognese, tacos or chicken schnitzel. They're *reassuring, nostalgic* and most of all, SUPER-YUM. But I also feel like they're in need of *a little updating*. Just a few tweaks to FRESHEN THINGS UP! Here are some of my modern, *vegie-forward spins* on the classics. You'll learn my clever ways to tie in MORE GOODNESS, all while in the comfort of familiar territory.

tofu banh mi

¼ cup (60ml/2 fl oz) apple cider vinegar
1 tablespoon coconut sugar
sea salt flakes
2 carrots, peeled and grated or shredded using
   a julienne peeler
2 long red chillies, sliced
1 tablespoon light-flavoured extra virgin olive oil
1 long baguette, cut into 4 rolls
   and halved lengthways
⅓ cup (100g/3½ oz) mayonnaise
1 cucumber, thinly sliced lengthways
½ cup (6g/¼ oz) coriander (cilantro) leaves
½ cup (8g/¼ oz) mint leaves
marinated tofu
2 tablespoons finely grated ginger
1 clove garlic, crushed
1 teaspoon finely grated lime rind
1 tablespoon lime juice
2 teaspoons honey
1 tablespoon soy sauce
1 tablespoon sriracha hot chilli sauce
450g (1 lb) firm tofu, sliced

To make the marinated tofu, place the ginger, garlic, lime rind and juice, honey, soy sauce and sriracha in a large bowl and mix to combine. Add the tofu and toss to coat. Allow to marinate for 30 minutes.

Place the vinegar, sugar and salt in a medium bowl and whisk to combine. Add the carrot and half the chilli and toss to combine.

Heat the oil in a large non-stick frying pan over medium-high heat. Cook the tofu for 3–4 minutes each side or until golden.

Spread each roll with mayonnaise and fill with the cucumber, pickled carrot mixture, tofu, coriander, mint and the remaining chilli. **MAKES 4**

cook's note
The combination of flavours in this Vietnamese classic is seriously addictive. I'm in love with the tofu variation, but you can marinate and pan-fry sliced chicken breast or pork fillet if you prefer.

crunchy quinoa schnitzels with buttermilk slaw

1 egg
2 tablespoons milk
1 cup (100g/3½ oz) quinoa flakes
¼ cup (30g/1 oz) store-bought dukkah
⅓ cup (55g/2 oz) almonds, finely chopped
⅓ cup (25g/1 oz) finely grated parmesan
sea salt and cracked black pepper
500g (1 lb 2 oz) chicken breast fillets, cut into
   2.5cm (1 in) slices
extra virgin olive oil, for drizzling
buttermilk slaw
¼ cup (60ml/2 fl oz) buttermilk
1 tablespoon lemon juice
1 teaspoon Dijon mustard
sea salt and cracked black pepper
4 cups (360g/12¾ oz) finely shredded green cabbage
1 bulb fennel (180g/6½ oz), trimmed and finely sliced
1 Granny Smith (green) apple (120g/4¼ oz),
   finely sliced

Preheat oven grill (broiler) to high. Line a large baking tray with non-stick baking paper.

Place the egg in a medium shallow bowl and lightly whisk. Add the milk and whisk to combine.

Place the quinoa flakes, dukkah, almonds, parmesan, salt and pepper in a large bowl and mix to combine.

Dip the chicken strips in the egg mixture, then press firmly into the quinoa mixture to coat. Place on the tray and drizzle with oil. Place the tray on a middle shelf of the oven and cook for 5 minutes. Turn and cook for a further 5 minutes or until the crust is golden brown and crunchy and the chicken is cooked through.

To make the buttermilk slaw, place the buttermilk, lemon juice, mustard, salt and pepper in a large bowl. Add the cabbage, fennel and apple and toss gently to coat in the dressing.

Divide the schnitzels between serving plates and serve with the slaw. **SERVES 4**

cook's note
My kids request schnitzel all the time, so I make them this version with quinoa and nuts in place of breadcrumbs. The tender chicken strips are grilled in the oven instead of shallow-fried in a pan – it's less mess, plus the crust goes super crunchy.

the best vegie burgers

1 x 400g (14 oz) can black beans or red kidney beans,
  rinsed and drained
1 cup (150g/5¼ oz) firmly packed grated carrot
  (about 1 carrot)
1 cup (150g/5¼ oz) firmly packed grated beetroot
  (about 1 medium beetroot)
2 tablespoons black chia seeds
½ cup (140g/5 oz) crunchy peanut butter
  or hulled tahini
1 teaspoon ground cumin
1 teaspoon smoky sweet paprika
½ cup (12g/½ oz) flat-leaf parsley leaves
sea salt and cracked black pepper
2 tablespoons extra virgin olive oil
4 seeded bread rolls or burger buns, halved
4 cos (Romaine) lettuce leaves
8 small slices cheddar
2 tomatoes, sliced
⅓ cup (100g/3½ oz) mayonnaise or relish
4 large dill pickles, quartered lengthways

Place the beans in a large bowl and press with a fork
until roughly mashed. Add the carrot, beetroot, chia
seeds, peanut butter, cumin, paprika, parsley, salt and
pepper and mix to combine. Divide the mixture into
4 equal portions and shape into patties.

Heat a large non-stick frying pan over medium-high
heat. Add the oil and the patties and cook for 5 minutes
each side or until golden brown.

Divide the bun bases between serving plates and
top with the lettuce, vegie patties, cheddar, tomato
and mayonnaise. Sandwich with the tops of the buns
and serve with the pickles. **MAKES 4**

cook's note
What's a beach day or balmy
summer's evening without a
burger every now and again?
Meat-free doesn't have to
mean flavour-free... in fact,
my boys often prefer these
vegie variations to traditional
beef burgers. You can cook
these patties on a char-grill
pan or barbecue, if you wish.

chilli, lime and ginger thai tofu cakes

35g (1¼ oz) ginger, peeled and roughly chopped
1 clove garlic, roughly chopped
6 coriander (cilantro) roots, trimmed
6 kaffir lime leaves
1–2 long red chillies, halved
2 tablespoons fish sauce or coconut aminos
2 tablespoons raw caster (superfine) sugar
750g (1 lb 10 oz) firm tofu, roughly chopped
2 tablespoons brown rice flour
1 cup (12g/½ oz) coriander (cilantro) leaves
sesame seeds, for sprinkling
extra virgin olive oil, for drizzling
mixed salad greens, to serve
6 spears asparagus, thinly sliced into ribbons
1 long green chilli, chopped, for sprinkling
thai dipping sauce
2 tablespoons fish sauce or coconut aminos
2 tablespoons lime juice
1 tablespoon dark brown sugar or palm sugar

Preheat oven to 200°C (400°F). Line a large baking tray with non-stick baking paper.

Place the ginger, garlic, coriander roots, lime leaves, red chilli, fish sauce and caster sugar in a food processor and process into a coarse paste. Add the tofu, flour and coriander leaves and process to combine.

Shape ¼-cup portions of the mixture into patties (see *cook's note*) and place on the tray. Sprinkle with sesame seeds and drizzle with oil. Bake for 15 minutes or until firm and light golden.

To make the Thai dipping sauce, place the fish sauce, lime juice and sugar in a small bowl and mix to combine.

Divide salad greens between serving plates and top with the asparagus, tofu cakes and green chilli. Serve with the dipping sauce. **MAKES 14**

cook's note
One of my little tricks when shaping a mixture like this into patties, fishcakes or meatballs is to use slightly wet hands. Any stickiness or dryness will disappear!

chipotle chicken and cauliflower tacos

1 x 215g (7½ oz) can chipotle chillies in adobo sauce,
    chillies finely chopped and sauce reserved
1 tablespoon maple syrup
2 cloves garlic, finely chopped
2 tablespoons extra virgin olive oil
500g (1 lb 2 oz) chicken thigh fillets, trimmed
    and quartered
500g (1 lb 2 oz) cauliflower florets (about 1 head)
sea salt and cracked black pepper
12 small corn tortillas (330g/11½ oz), lightly toasted
3⅓ cups (300g/10½ oz) finely shredded
    purple cabbage
1 cup (12g/½ oz) coriander (cilantro) sprigs
pickled red onions (see *recipe*, page 226), to serve
lime wedges, to serve
lime dressing
½ cup (140g/5 oz) plain Greek-style (thick) yoghurt
1½ tablespoons lime juice
sea salt and cracked black pepper

Preheat oven to 220°C (425°F). Line 2 oven trays with
non-stick baking paper.

Place the chopped chillies and reserved adobo sauce
in a large bowl. Add the maple syrup, garlic and oil and
mix to combine.

Place the chicken in a separate large bowl and top
with half the chipotle mixture. Toss to coat.

Add the cauliflower to the remaining chipotle mixture
and toss to coat.

Transfer the chicken and cauliflower to the trays and
sprinkle with salt and pepper. Roast for 20 minutes or
until the cauliflower is just charred on the edges, the
chicken is cooked through and the sauce has thickened.

To make the lime dressing, place the yoghurt, lime
juice, salt and pepper in a small bowl and mix to combine.

Fill the warm tortillas with the cabbage, chicken,
cauliflower and coriander. Drizzle with the lime dressing
and serve with pickled onion and lime wedges. **SERVES 4**

cook's notes

At my house, I put all the
fillings on the table and let
everyone build their own
tacos – they can choose their
favourite combinations, so
it's more fun and less fuss.

To make these tacos meat
free, simply leave out the
chicken and double the
amount of cauliflower.

chicken caesar salad with crispy kale

500g (1 lb 2 oz) kale (about 10 stalks), stems removed
   and leaves torn
¼ cup (60ml/2 fl oz) extra virgin olive oil
sea salt and cracked black pepper
400g (14 oz) wholemeal (whole-wheat) sourdough
   bread (about half a loaf), torn into 2.5cm (1 in) pieces
6 cloves garlic, skin on
2 x 180g (6¼ oz) chicken breast fillets, trimmed
½ cup (140g/5 oz) plain Greek-style (thick) yoghurt
¼ cup (75g/2½ oz) mayonnaise
⅓ cup (8g/¼ oz) flat-leaf parsley leaves, finely chopped
¼ cup (60ml/2 fl oz) lemon juice
2 teaspoons Dijon mustard
1 baby cos (Romaine) lettuce (150g/5¼ oz),
   leaves separated
½ cup (40g/1½ oz) finely shaved parmesan

Preheat oven to 180°C (350°F). Line 2 large baking trays with non-stick baking paper. Place the kale in a large bowl and add 1 tablespoon of the oil. Sprinkle with salt and pepper and toss to combine. Divide between the trays, spread in a single layer and bake for 15 minutes or until very crispy. Allow to cool.

Increase the oven temperature to 200°C (400°F). Line a large baking tray with non-stick baking paper. Place the bread and garlic in a large bowl and add 1½ tablespoons of the oil. Toss to combine and spread over three-quarters of the tray. Place the chicken in the remaining space on the tray and drizzle with the remaining 2 teaspoons of oil. Sprinkle the tray with salt and pepper and roast for 20 minutes or until the bread is golden and the chicken is cooked through.

Squeeze the garlic from its skin into a small bowl and mash into a paste. Add the yoghurt, mayonnaise, parsley, lemon juice, mustard, salt and pepper and mix to combine.

Divide the kale, lettuce leaves, croutons and parmesan between serving bowls. Slice the chicken and arrange in the bowls. Drizzle with the dressing to serve. SERVES 4

cook's note
We all love classic Caesar salad for its signature flavours and textures, like creamy dressing, crunchy fresh lettuce and toasty croutons. My modern variation has all these elements – but with a lighter touch – plus I've added a nutrient boost of crispy kale.

vegie bolognese

2 tablespoons extra virgin olive oil

2 onions, finely chopped

1 x 400g (14 oz) can chickpeas (garbanzo beans),
   drained, rinsed and roughly chopped

½ cup (15g/½ oz) dried sliced porcini mushrooms

1 cup (250ml/8½ fl oz) boiling water

2½ cups (300g/10½ oz) coarsely grated pumpkin

1¼ cups (200g/7 oz) coarsely grated zucchini
   (courgette) (about 1 medium zucchini)

1 tablespoon oregano leaves

2 cloves garlic, crushed

2¾ cups (680ml/23 fl oz) tomato passata

1 x 400g (14 oz) can cherry tomatoes

1 tablespoon balsamic vinegar

sea salt and cracked black pepper

400g (14 oz) dried wholemeal (whole-wheat) pasta

basil leaves, to serve

finely grated parmesan, to serve

Place a large deep-sided frying pan over medium heat.
Add the oil, onion and chickpeas and cook for 10 minutes,
stirring occasionally, until the mixture is deep golden
in colour.

While the chickpeas are cooking, place the porcini
in a medium heatproof bowl and cover with the water.
Allow to soak for 15 minutes or until softened.

While the mushrooms are soaking, add the pumpkin,
zucchini, oregano and garlic to the pan and cook,
stirring, for 5 minutes.

Drain the mushrooms, reserving the soaking liquid,
finely chop and add them to the pan. Add the reserved
liquid, passata and tomatoes. Allow to simmer for
10 minutes or until the mixture has thickened. Add the
vinegar, salt and pepper and stir to combine.

While the sauce is simmering, cook the pasta in a
large saucepan of salted boiling water for 8–10 minutes
or until al dente. Drain and divide between serving
bowls. Top with the sauce and sprinkle with basil and
parmesan to serve. **SERVES 4**

cook's note

Hiding vegies in bolognese
is a not-so-well-kept secret
that most parents have been
in on for years! This recipe
takes that one step further.
I think you'll be surprised
how good this version of the
classic tastes. If nothing else,
it'll become your go-to for
meat-free Mondays.

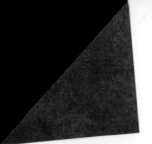

super-green ricotta rolls

1 tablespoon extra virgin olive oil
1 onion, finely chopped
480g (1 lb 1 oz) silverbeet (Swiss chard)
  (about 6 stalks), trimmed, leaves and stems chopped
1 clove garlic, crushed
1 cup (150g/5¼ oz) firmly packed grated pumpkin
300g (10½ oz) kale (about 6 stalks), stems removed
  and leaves finely chopped
1 cup (240g/8½ oz) fresh ricotta
2 teaspoons finely grated lemon rind
⅓ cup (8g/¼ oz) flat-leaf parsley leaves, finely chopped
⅓ cup (25g/1 oz) finely grated parmesan
sea salt and cracked black pepper
1 x 375g (13¼ oz) sheet frozen wholemeal (whole-wheat)
  butter puff pastry, thawed (see *cook's note*)
1 egg, lightly beaten

Place a large deep-sided non-stick frying pan over
medium-high heat. Add the oil, onion and silverbeet
stems and cook, stirring, for 4 minutes or until soft
and golden. Add the garlic and pumpkin and cook for
3 minutes or until soft. Add the silverbeet and kale
leaves and cook for 1 minute or until wilted.

Transfer the greens mixture to large a bowl. Add
the ricotta, lemon rind, parsley, parmesan, salt and
pepper and mix to combine. Refrigerate until cool.

Preheat oven to 220°C (425°F). Line a large baking
tray with non-stick baking paper. Cut the pastry
sheet in half to make 2 x 13.5cm x 18cm (5½ in x 7 in)
rectangles and place on the tray. Divide the greens
mixture between the pastry, arranging it in logs along
one of each long edge. Brush the other long edges
with the beaten egg and roll to enclose the filling.
Cut each roll in half to make 4 in total. Turn the rolls,
seam-side down, on the trays. Score the tops with a
sharp knife and brush with the remaining egg.

Bake for 25 minutes or until the pastry is puffed
and golden brown. Allow the rolls to cool on the
tray for 10 minutes before serving. **MAKES 4**

cook's note
You can buy frozen puff
pastry that's been made with
spelt flour, in 27cm x 36cm
(10½ in x 14 in) sheets, at
specialty food stores and
major greengrocers. If you
can't get a single 375g (13¼ oz)
sheet of butter puff pastry,
place 2 regular sheets of puff
pastry together, overlapping
by 4cm (1½ in). Using a rolling
pin, roll the sheets together to
secure, then trim the edges.

want you to *be inspired* to create your *old favourites* in a different way. Give them MORE CRUNCH, *more personality*, more colour and, in turn, MORE FLAVOUR.

thai beef salad

400g (14 oz) beef eye fillet, trimmed
2 teaspoons extra virgin olive oil
sea salt flakes, for sprinkling
2 small kohlrabi or fennel bulbs (350g/12¼ oz),
   trimmed and shredded
2 small Granny Smith (green) apples (260g/9 oz),
   thinly sliced
2 cups (40g/1½ oz) Thai basil leaves
250g (8¾ oz) rocket (arugula)
4 baby cucumbers, quartered lengthways
nam jim dressing
2 long red chillies, seeded and roughly chopped
1 clove garlic, roughly chopped
2 tablespoons lime juice
2 tablespoons water
1½ tablespoons light brown sugar
1 tablespoon fish sauce or coconut aminos
⅓ cup (50g/1¾ oz) roasted cashews

Preheat oven to 180°C (350°F). Line a baking tray with
non-stick baking paper.

Drizzle the beef with oil and rub to coat. Sprinkle with
salt. Heat a small non-stick frying pan over high heat.
Sear the beef for 2 minutes on each of the sides until
evenly browned all over. Transfer to the tray and roast
for 10 minutes for medium rare or until cooked to your
liking. Allow the beef to rest for 10 minutes. Slice into
thin pieces.

To make the nam jim dressing, place the chilli, garlic,
lime juice, water, sugar and fish sauce in a small food
processor and process until finely chopped. Add the
cashews and pulse until the nuts are finely chopped.

Divide the beef, kohlrabi, apple, basil, rocket and
cucumber between serving plates and drizzle with the
dressing to serve. **SERVES 4**

cook's note
Why a beef recipe in the
middle of a vegetable-inspired
book? I wanted to acknowledge
the way I cook at home. Some
days my boys and I feel like
eating red meat, other times
it may just be one or two of
us. I try to be flexible with
swapping meat for tofu or
more veg and hope these
recipes give you the confidence
and freedom to do the same.

crispy buttermilk chicken with sprout and celeriac slaw

2⅓ cups (580ml/20 fl oz) buttermilk
1½ teaspoons sea salt flakes
6 x 200g (7 oz) chicken thigh fillets, trimmed
2 tablespoons extra virgin olive oil
1½ cups (280g/10 oz) wholemeal (whole-wheat)
   spelt flour
1 tablespoon thyme leaves
1 teaspoon Chinese five-spice powder
2 teaspoons smoky sweet paprika
¼ cup (75g/2½ oz) mayonnaise
¼ cup (70g/2½ oz) plain Greek-style (thick) yoghurt
juice and finely grated rind of half a lime
sea salt flakes, extra
200g (7 oz) Brussels sprouts (about 8 sprouts), shaved
150g (5¼ oz) celeriac (celery root), peeled and shredded
¼ cup (6g/¼ oz) dill sprigs
1 green onion (scallion), finely sliced
toasted sourdough bread slices, to serve

Place the buttermilk and 1 teaspoon of the salt in a large non-reactive container (see *cook's note*) and whisk to combine. Add the chicken and toss to coat. Cover and refrigerate for 2–6 hours or overnight.

Preheat oven to 180°C (350°F). Brush the oil over a large baking tray. Place the flour, thyme, five-spice, paprika and the remaining ½ teaspoon salt in a large bowl and mix to combine. Remove 1 piece of chicken from the buttermilk, shaking off any excess. Press both sides into the flour mixture and shake well to remove any excess. Place on the tray, allowing room to brown evenly. Repeat with the remaining chicken and flour mixture.

Bake for 25 minutes or until browned. Turn and bake for a further 25 minutes or until cooked through and crisp.

While the chicken is baking, place the mayonnaise, yoghurt, lime juice and rind in a large bowl. Sprinkle with a little extra salt and whisk to combine. Add the sprouts, celeriac, dill and onion and toss to combine.

Divide the sourdough between serving plates and top with the slaw and chicken to serve. **SERVES 4**

cook's note
When marinating meats or vegetables in an acidic mixture such as a brine, buttermilk or vinegar, it's best to use a non-reactive container – glass, ceramic or plastic will all work well.

super-green lasagne

1 leek, trimmed, halved lengthways and shredded
2 tablespoons extra virgin olive oil
1kg (2 lb 3 oz) fresh ricotta
1 cup (250ml/8½ fl oz) milk
1½ cups (120g/4¼ oz) finely grated parmesan
1 tablespoon finely grated lemon rind
sea salt and cracked black pepper
600g (1 lb 5 oz) kale (about 12 stalks), stems removed,
    leaves blanched (see *cook's note*)
960g (2 lb 2 oz) silverbeet (Swiss chard) (about 12 stalks),
    stems removed, leaves blanched (see *cook's note*)
450g (1 lb) fresh lasagne sheets
220g (7¾ oz) fresh mozzarella, torn
broccoli pesto
500g (1 lb 2 oz) broccoli florets (about 2 heads)
3 cups (60g/2 oz) basil leaves
½ cup (80g/2¾ oz) pine nuts
2 cloves garlic, crushed
¼ cup (60ml/2 fl oz) lemon juice
2 tablespoons extra virgin olive oil

Preheat oven to 180°C (350°F). Lightly oil a 24cm x 38cm
(9½ in x 15 in) 4-litre-capacity (135 fl oz) baking dish.
Place the leek and oil in a small bowl and toss to coat.

To make the broccoli pesto, place the broccoli, basil,
pine nuts and garlic in a food processor and process until
fine. Add the lemon juice and oil and process into a pesto.

Place the ricotta and milk in a large bowl and whisk
until smooth. Add ¾ cup (60g/2 oz) of the parmesan,
the lemon rind, salt and pepper and mix to combine.

Line the base of the dish with half the kale and half the
silverbeet. Top with a layer of lasagne sheets, trimming
to fit. Spread with half the pesto. Cover with lasagne
sheets then spread with half the ricotta mixture. Cover
with lasagne sheets. Repeat the layering, using the
remaining greens, lasagne sheets and pesto, finishing
with ricotta mixture. Sprinkle with the mozzarella, the
remaining ¾ cup (60g/2 oz) of parmesan and the leek.
Bake for 45-50 minutes or until golden brown. **SERVES 8**

cook's note
I find it easiest to blanch the
leaves in a large saucepan.
Simply cover them with
boiling water and allow to
stand for 1 minute. Once
you've drained them,
arrange the leaves flat on
a tray or board so they're
ready to layer into the
lasagne as you need them.

char-grilled steak and mushroom open sandwiches

500g (1 lb 2 oz) beef rump steak, trimmed
4 large flat mushrooms (400g/14 oz), stems trimmed
300g (10½ oz) orange sweet potato (kumara), very
   thinly sliced
⅓ cup (80ml/2¾ fl oz) extra virgin olive oil
sea salt and cracked black pepper
4 thick slices sourdough bread
rocket (arugula) leaves, to serve
dill pickles, halved, to serve
green tahini sauce
¼ cup (70g/2½ oz) hulled tahini
1 cup (16g/½ oz) mint leaves
1 cup (12g/½ oz) coriander (cilantro) leaves
¼ cup (60ml/2 fl oz) lemon juice
¼ cup (60ml/2 fl oz) water
1 clove garlic, crushed
sea salt and cracked black pepper

To make the green tahini sauce, place the tahini, mint, coriander, lemon juice, water, garlic, salt and pepper in a blender and blend until smooth.

Preheat a char-grill pan or barbecue over high heat. Drizzle the steak, mushrooms and sweet potato with 1 tablespoon each of the oil to coat. Sprinkle with salt and pepper. Cook the steak and mushrooms for 4 minutes each side or until cooked to your liking. Allow the steak to rest for 5 minutes, then slice.

While the steak is resting, cook the sweet potato for 1 minute each side or until tender. Brush the bread with the remaining 1 tablespoon of oil and cook for 30 seconds each side or until well toasted.

Divide the toast between serving plates and top each with a mushroom. Stack with rocket and drizzle with the green tahini sauce. Top with the sliced steak and sweet potato. Sprinkle with salt and pepper and serve with pickles. **SERVES 4**

cook's note
Depending on my mood, I'll sometimes swap out the steak altogether in this recipe and double the quantity of mushrooms – they're a super-tasty alternative to beef.

vegetable dumplings

2 teaspoons sesame oil
1 tablespoon finely grated ginger
1 clove garlic, crushed
3 green onions (scallions), finely chopped
1 cup (40g/1½ oz) finely shredded English spinach leaves
1 cup (50g/1¾ oz) finely shredded kale leaves
1 cup (120g/4¼ oz) frozen peas, thawed
¼ cup (50g/1¾ oz) finely chopped water chestnuts
100g (3½ oz) firm silken tofu, finely chopped
2 tablespoons chopped coriander (cilantro) leaves
½ teaspoon sea salt flakes
30 gow gee or wonton wrappers (275g/9¾ oz)
1 tablespoon extra virgin olive oil
⅓ cup (80ml/2¾ fl oz) water
steamed gai lan (Chinese broccoli), to serve
toasted sesame seeds, to serve
chilli sauce and soy sauce or coconut aminos, to serve

Heat a large non-stick frying pan over medium-high heat. Add the sesame oil, ginger, garlic and onion and cook, stirring, for 1 minute. Add the spinach and kale and cook for 2 minutes or until wilted. Place the peas in a medium bowl and lightly crush with a fork. Add the peas, chestnuts, tofu, coriander and salt to the pan and stir until combined. Remove from the heat.

Arrange the gow gee wrappers on a clean surface. Place 1 heaped teaspoon of the mixture in the centre of each wrapper. Brush the edges of the wrappers with a little water, fold to enclose and pinch to seal.

Heat 2 teaspoons of the olive oil in a medium non-stick frying pan over medium heat. Add half the dumplings, flat-side down, and cook for 3 minutes. Add 2 tablespoons of the water, cover with a tight-fitting lid and simmer for 3 minutes. Uncover and cook for a further 3–4 minutes or until the water evaporates and the dumplings are golden and crispy. Repeat with the remaining oil, dumplings and water. Divide the dumplings and greens between serving plates and sprinkle with sesame seeds. Serve with chilli and soy sauce. **MAKES 30**

cook's note
I like dumplings crispy and golden from the pan, but if you prefer steamed, just place them, in batches, in a lightly oiled bamboo steamer over a pan of simmering water. Steam for 10–12 minutes or until cooked through.

sweet potato pizzas

1kg (2 lb 3 oz) orange sweet potato (kumara), peeled
   and roughly chopped
1½ cups (180g/6¼ oz) almond meal (ground almonds)
½ cup (80g/2¾ oz) buckwheat flour
2 eggs
160g (5½ oz) baby cavolo nero (Tuscan kale) leaves,
   stems trimmed
1 tablespoon finely shredded lemon rind
150g (5¼ oz) goat's cheese, sliced
1 long red chilli, sliced
extra virgin olive oil, for drizzling

Preheat oven to 200°C (400°F). Line 2 x 33cm (13 in)
round pizza trays with non-stick baking paper.

Place the sweet potato in a steamer and position
over a saucepan of boiling water. Steam until tender.
Transfer the sweet potato to a large bowl and mash
until smooth. Allow to cool slightly.

Add the almond meal, flour and eggs to the potato
and mix to combine.

Divide the sweet potato dough between the trays and
spread evenly to make 2 bases. Bake for 25 minutes
or until the bases are dry to the touch and the edges
are golden.

Top the bases with the cavolo nero, lemon rind, goat's
cheese and chilli. Drizzle with oil and bake for a further
10 minutes. Slice to serve. **SERVES 4**

cook's notes
These bases are a great
gluten-free alternative to
regular pizza dough, plus
the sweet potato lends
them extra flavour.

You can top the pizzas with
your favourite green leaves
and crumble or grate over
whichever cheese you like.
Serve them straight from the
oven so they stay crunchy.

vegetable mac and cheese

300g (10½ oz) dried wholemeal (whole-wheat)
  macaroni or penne
600g (1 lb 5 oz) cauliflower florets
500g (1 lb 2 oz) pumpkin, peeled and roughly chopped
2 zucchinis (courgettes), roughly chopped
1 tablespoon thyme leaves
2 cups (500ml/17 fl oz) milk
⅔ cup (50g/1¾ oz) finely grated parmesan
⅔ cup (80g/2¾ oz) finely grated cheddar
sea salt and cracked black pepper
16 sage leaves
1 tablespoon extra virgin olive oil
300g (10½ oz) wholemeal (whole-wheat) bread, torn

Preheat oven to 180°C (350°F). Lightly grease a 22cm
x 28cm (8½ in x 11 in) 2.75-litre-capacity (93 fl oz) baking
dish. Cook the pasta in a large saucepan of salted boiling
water for 8 minutes or until al dente. Drain and set aside.

Place the cauliflower, pumpkin, zucchini and thyme in a
large saucepan over medium heat. Top with the milk and
cover with a tight-fitting lid. Simmer for 12–15 minutes or
until soft. Remove from the heat and allow to cool slightly.
Using a stick blender, blend the vegetable mixture until
smooth. Add the parmesan, cheddar, salt and pepper
and stir to combine.

Place the sage and oil in a small bowl and toss to coat.
Place the pasta in the dish and top with the vegetable
puree. Sprinkle with the torn bread, sage leaves and
salt and bake for 25 minutes or until golden. SERVES 4-6

cook's note
We all need comfort food
from time to time, but I like
to think it can still be made
with feel-good ingredients.
My vegetable answer to
béchamel sauce brings new
life to everyone's favourite
cosy classic.

CHAPTER TWO

bowls

of

goodness

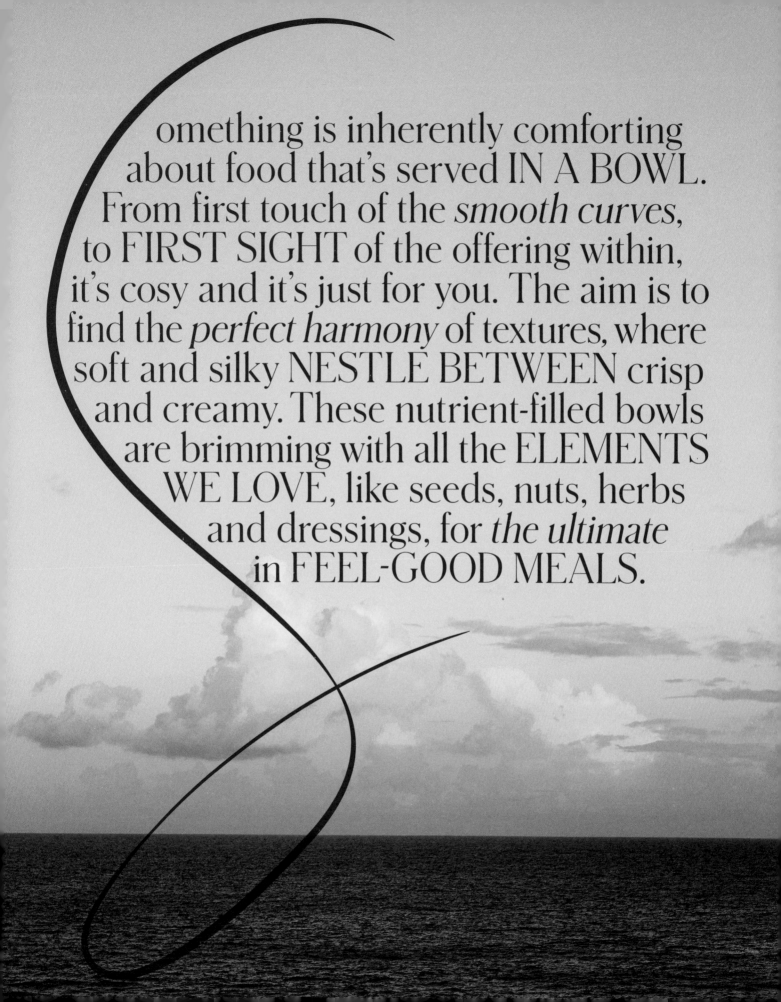

omething is inherently comforting about food that's served IN A BOWL. From first touch of the *smooth curves*, to FIRST SIGHT of the offering within, it's cosy and it's just for you. The aim is to find the *perfect harmony* of textures, where soft and silky NESTLE BETWEEN crisp and creamy. These nutrient-filled bowls are brimming with all the ELEMENTS WE LOVE, like seeds, nuts, herbs and dressings, for *the ultimate* in FEEL-GOOD MEALS.

cheat's chilli cashew tofu larb

2 teaspoons extra virgin olive oil
2 tablespoons finely grated ginger
⅓ cup (100g/3½ oz) Asian chilli jam or paste
¼ cup (60ml/2 fl oz) fish sauce or coconut aminos
¼ cup (55g/2 oz) raw caster (superfine) sugar
500g (1 lb 2 oz) firm tofu, drained and crumbled
   (see *cook's note*)
⅓ cup (80ml/2¾ fl oz) lime juice
12 baby cos (Romaine) lettuce leaves
2 cucumbers, chopped lengthways
¾ cup (110g/4 oz) roasted salted cashews,
   roughly chopped
½ cup (10g/¼ oz) Thai basil leaves
½ cup (6g/¼ oz) coriander (cilantro) leaves
lime cheeks, to serve

Place a large non-stick frying pan over medium-high heat.
Add the oil, ginger and chilli jam and cook for 3 minutes
or until fragrant. Add 2 tablespoons of the fish sauce,
2 tablespoons of the sugar and the tofu. Cook, stirring,
for 4 minutes or until the tofu is heated through. Add
¼ cup (60ml/2 fl oz) of the lime juice and stir to combine.

   Place the remaining 1 tablespoon of each of the fish
sauce, sugar and lime juice in a small bowl and mix to
dissolve the sugar.

   Divide the lettuce, cucumber and cashews between
serving plates and spoon the tofu into serving bowls.
Top with the basil and coriander and serve with the
dressing and lime cheeks. **SERVES 4**

cook's note
You can swap the tofu for
500g (1 lb 2 oz) chicken
or pork mince if you like.
Meat will need more time
in the pan than tofu, to be
sure it's cooked through.

spring greens bowls

600g (1 lb 5 oz) broccoli florets (about 2 heads)
1 tablespoon extra virgin olive oil
sea salt and cracked black pepper
150g (5¼ oz) sugar snap peas, trimmed
1 cup (140g/5 oz) frozen shelled edamame beans
2 tablespoons hemp seeds or sesame seeds, toasted
2 small avocados, quartered lengthways
¼ cup (70g/2½ oz) store-bought pickled ginger
1 x quantity green dressing (see *recipe*, page 228)

In 2 batches, place the broccoli in a food processor and process until it resembles rice. Heat a large deep-sided frying pan over medium-high heat. Add the oil, broccoli, salt and pepper and cook, stirring, for 3 minutes or until the broccoli is just tender. Divide between serving bowls and allow to cool.

Place the peas and edamame in a large heatproof bowl. Cover with boiling water and allow to stand for 5 minutes. Drain and rinse under cold running water. Slice the peas lengthways.

Place the hemp seeds on a small tray and press one edge of each avocado quarter into the seeds to coat.

Top the broccoli rice with the peas, edamame, avocado and ginger. Drizzle with the dressing to serve. **SERVES 4**

cook's notes
Add some more fuel to your nourishing bowl if you wish, by way of a peeled and halved soft-boiled egg.

You can use cauliflower in place of the broccoli in this recipe, if you prefer.

crunchy raw pad thai

250g (8¾ oz) Chinese cabbage (about one-quarter
  of a cabbage), finely shredded
3 carrots, peeled and shredded (see *cook's notes*)
2 zucchinis (courgettes), shredded (see *cook's notes*)
2 long red chillies, seeds removed and shredded
4 green onions (scallions), shredded
⅔ cup (8g/¼ oz) coriander (cilantro) leaves
⅔ cup (10g/¼ oz) mint leaves
¾ cup (110g/4 oz) roasted salted cashews,
  roughly chopped
lime wedges, to serve
pad thai dressing
⅓ cup (80g/2¾ oz) almond or cashew butter
¼ cup (60ml/2 fl oz) lime juice
2 tablespoons soy sauce or coconut aminos
2 tablespoons coconut sugar
1 tablespoon finely grated ginger

Place the cabbage, carrot, zucchini, chilli and half
the onion in a large bowl. Add the coriander and mint
and toss to combine.

To make the pad Thai dressing, place the almond
butter, lime juice, soy sauce, sugar and ginger in a
medium bowl and whisk to combine.

Divide the raw pad Thai between serving bowls and
sprinkle with the cashews and remaining onion. Top
with the dressing and serve with lime wedges. **SERVES 4**

cook's notes
I've used a julienne peeler
to shred the carrot and
zucchini, but if you don't
have one, you can use a
regular peeler to make
thicker vegetable ribbons.

If you'd like to add something
extra to your own personal
bowl of raw vegie pad Thai,
there are lots of options to
choose from. You could throw
in some cooked rice noodles,
add 100g (3½ oz) crispy-fried
firm tofu, shred 120g (4¼ oz)
cooked chicken into your
bowl or even stir through
120g (4¼ oz) seared salmon
– just flake it into large pieces.

pasta with broccoli and lemon cashew-cream sauce

400g (14 oz) dried wholemeal (whole-wheat) spaghetti
300g (10½ oz) broccoli florets (about 1 head)
½ cup (10g/¼ oz) small basil leaves
1 tablespoon finely shredded lemon rind
lemon cashew-cream sauce
1 cup (150g/5¼ oz) raw cashews
2 cups (500ml/17 fl oz) boiling water
1 cup (250ml/8½ fl oz) good-quality vegetable stock
¼ cup (60ml/2 fl oz) lemon juice
sea salt and cracked black pepper

To make the lemon cashew-cream sauce, place the cashews in a medium heatproof bowl and cover with the boiling water. Allow to stand for 30 minutes. Drain the cashews well and place them in a blender. Add the stock, lemon juice, salt and pepper and blend until very smooth.

Cook the pasta in a large saucepan of salted boiling water for 6 minutes. Add the broccoli and cook for a further 4 minutes or until the pasta is al dente and the broccoli is just tender. Drain the pasta and broccoli and immediately return to the warm saucepan. Add the cashew-cream sauce and toss to combine.

Divide the pasta between serving bowls and top with the basil and lemon rind to serve. **SERVES 4**

cook's note
You can finish this pasta with finely grated parmesan and some extra cracked black pepper – they're great flavours with the creamy lemon sauce.

If the cashew-cream sauce is too thick, just add some extra vegie stock (or a little of the pasta's cooking water) to thin it to a creamy consistency.

sushi bowls

1⅓ cups (185g/6½ oz) frozen shelled edamame beans
4 cups (800g/1 lb 12 oz) cooked brown rice
2 small avocados, quartered lengthways
2 cucumbers, thinly sliced
¼ cup (70g/2½ oz) store-bought pickled ginger
2 tablespoons white or black sesame seeds, toasted
2 sheets toasted nori, finely shredded
⅓ cup (30g/1 oz) wasabi peas, chopped (optional)
wasabi dressing
¼ cup (60ml/2 fl oz) mirin (Japanese rice wine)
2 tablespoons white miso paste (shiro)
2 teaspoons wasabi paste (see *cook's notes*)
2 teaspoons raw caster (superfine) sugar

To make the wasabi dressing, place the mirin, miso paste, wasabi paste and sugar in a small bowl and mix to combine.

Place the edamame in a medium heatproof bowl and cover with boiling water. Allow to stand for 4 minutes or until tender. Drain and rinse under cold running water.

Divide the rice, avocado, cucumber and edamame between serving bowls. Top with the ginger and sesame seeds. Spoon the wasabi dressing over and sprinkle with the nori and wasabi peas to serve. **SERVES 4**

cook's notes
Just like when I'm in my favourite sushi bar, I love to choose the combinations I'm craving (and so do my kids!). You can customise your sushi bowl by adding 120g (4¼ oz) chopped sashimi-grade salmon or tuna per serving... or maybe you'd prefer 5 cooked and peeled prawns (shrimp)? Smoked salmon works well too, you'd need 3 slices per bowl. Other tasty options include 80g (2¾ oz) thinly sliced rare-roasted beef fillet or 80g (2¾ oz) shredded cooked chicken per serving.

If you like a little more heat, you could add 1–2 teaspoons of extra wasabi paste to the dressing.

coconut cucumber-noodle bowls with crispy fish

4 cucumbers (520g/1 lb 2 oz), shredded
   using a julienne peeler (see *cook's notes*)
4 celery stalks (400g/14 oz), shredded
   using a julienne peeler (see *cook's notes*)
2 cups (32g/1 oz) mint leaves
2 cups (24g/¾ oz) coriander (cilantro) leaves
½ cup (25g/¾ oz) toasted coconut flakes
4 x 90g (3 oz) firm white fish fillets, skin on
   (see *cook's notes*)
2 teaspoons sea salt flakes
1 teaspoon extra virgin olive oil
4 kaffir lime leaves, finely shredded
coconut dressing
⅔ cup (160ml/5½ fl oz) coconut cream
2 tablespoons lime juice
2 teaspoons fish sauce or coconut aminos
1 tablespoon raw caster (superfine) sugar

To make the coconut dressing, place the coconut cream, lime juice, fish sauce and sugar in a medium bowl and whisk to dissolve the sugar.

Place the cucumber, celery, mint, coriander and coconut flakes in a large bowl and toss to combine. Add the dressing and toss to coat.

Dry the fish well using absorbent kitchen paper. Sprinkle the skin with the salt. Heat the oil in a large non-stick frying pan over high heat. Place the fish, skin-side down, in the pan and cover with a sheet of non-stick baking paper. Top with a heavy pan to weigh the fish down and cook for 3 minutes or until the skin is crisp and golden. Remove the weight and paper, turn the fish and cook for a further 1 minute.

Divide the salad between serving bowls and top with the fish and lime leaves to serve. **SERVES 4**

cook's notes

I've used whiting fillets here, but you can use any fish you prefer.

I've used a julienne peeler to shred the cucumber and celery. If you don't have one, you can use a regular peeler to make vegetable ribbons.

Sometimes I'll reserve half the herbs and half the dressing and place them on the table, so everyone can add their own to serve.

spicy peanut cauliflower-rice bowls

800g (1 lb 12 oz) cauliflower florets (about 1 large head)
¼ cup (60ml/2 fl oz) extra virgin olive oil
2 long red chillies, chopped
1 cup (140g/5 oz) roasted unsalted peanuts,
   roughly chopped
250g (8¾ oz) green beans, halved lengthways
   and blanched
2 zucchinis (courgettes), shredded using
   a julienne peeler
2 green onions (scallions), thinly sliced
peanut dressing
⅓ cup (90g/3 oz) crunchy peanut butter
⅓ cup (80ml/2¾ fl oz) coconut milk
1 tablespoon soy sauce or coconut aminos
2 teaspoons raw caster (superfine) sugar
2 tablespoons lime juice

To make the peanut dressing, place the peanut butter, coconut milk, soy sauce, sugar and lime juice in a medium bowl, whisk to dissolve the sugar and set aside.

In 2 batches, place the cauliflower in a food processor and process until it resembles rice.

Heat the oil in a large non-stick frying-pan over medium-high heat. Add the chilli and cook, stirring, for 2 minutes or until fragrant. Add the peanuts and cook for 1 minute. Add the cauliflower rice and cook, stirring, for 4 minutes or until just soft.

Divide the mixture between serving bowls and top with the beans, zucchini and onion. Serve with the peanut dressing. **SERVES 4**

cook's note
For a satay chicken variation on these bowls, you can grill 2 chicken breast fillets until they're tender and cooked through, slice them and add a few strips to each serving.

The trick with *these bowls*, unlike a SALAD OR STIR-FRY, is to keep things *a bit separate*. That way, while you're eating, you can choose to scoop up the PERFECT MIX of tangy and crunchy, *silky and smooth* or SWEET AND SPICY – yum!

crispy sprout bowls with honey tahini dressing

800g (1 lb 12 oz) Brussels sprouts (about 40 sprouts),
   trimmed and halved
2 leeks, trimmed and finely shredded into
   8cm (3 in) lengths
¼ cup (60ml/2 fl oz) extra virgin olive oil
sea salt and cracked black pepper
2 firm pears, thinly sliced lengthways
4 cups (100g/3½ oz) mixed salad leaves
   (see *cook's note*)
ground sumac, for sprinkling
salted honey walnuts
1 cup (100g/3½ oz) walnuts
1 tablespoon honey
½ teaspoon sea salt flakes
honey tahini dressing
½ cup (125ml/4¼ fl oz) lemon juice
⅓ cup (90g/3 oz) hulled tahini
2 tablespoons honey
2 tablespoons water
sea salt and cracked black pepper

Preheat oven to 200°C (400°F). Line 2 large baking
trays with non-stick baking paper.

Place the sprouts and leek in a large bowl, add the
oil and toss to combine. Spread over 1 of the trays and
sprinkle with salt and pepper. Roast for 20 minutes or
until the sprouts are dark golden and tender.

While the sprouts are roasting, make the salted honey
walnuts. Place the walnuts, honey and salt in a medium
bowl and mix to combine. Spread the walnut mixture
over the remaining tray and roast, on a lower rack of
the oven, for 8 minutes or until golden and caramelised.
Allow to cool on the tray.

To make the honey tahini dressing, place the lemon
juice, tahini, honey, water, salt and pepper in a medium
bowl and whisk until smooth.

Divide the sprout mixture between serving bowls and
top with the pear and salad leaves. Drizzle with dressing
and sprinkle with sumac and the walnuts to serve. **SERVES 4**

cook's note
My simple trick for stepping
things up in the salad stakes?
Switch up your leaves. I've
used a mix of beetroot leaves
and red-veined sorrel here,
which are sold loose at most
greengrocers. They bring their
colour and a lovely sweet-sharp
flavour to this bowl. You can
use your favourite mixed
leaves or try something new!

miso-roasted autumn vegetable bowls

1 medium eggplant (aubergine) (300g/10½ oz),
   cut into 4cm (1½ in) pieces
1 medium orange sweet potato (kumara) (400g/14 oz),
   cut into 2cm (¾ in) pieces
3 cups (480g/1 lb) cooked freekeh or brown rice
2 green onions (scallions), thinly sliced
4 red radishes, thinly sliced
2 cups (50g/1¾ oz) baby spinach leaves
sliced green onion (scallion), extra, to serve
sesame seeds, toasted, to serve
miso dressing
½ cup (110g/4 oz) white miso paste (shiro)
½ cup (125ml/4¼ fl oz) rice wine vinegar
½ cup (125ml/4¼ fl oz) mirin (Japanese rice wine)
2 tablespoons water
2 tablespoons raw caster (superfine) sugar

Preheat oven to 200°C (400°F). Line a large baking tray
with non-stick baking paper.

To make the miso dressing, place the miso paste, rice
wine vinegar, mirin, water and sugar in a large bowl.
Whisk to combine and set aside.

Place the eggplant and sweet potato in a separate
large bowl and add three-quarters of the miso dressing.
Toss to coat and transfer the mixture to the tray. Roast,
stirring halfway, for 30 minutes or until the vegetables
are golden and soft.

Add the freekeh and onion to the remaining miso
dressing and mix to combine (see *cook's notes*). Divide
between serving bowls and top with the radish, spinach
and miso-roasted vegetables. Sprinkle with extra onion
and sesame seeds to serve. **SERVES 4**

cook's notes

For a variation on this vegie
bowl, brush fillets of fish or
chicken with teriyaki sauce
and grill them until golden
and cooked through. Slice
and add to each serving.

If you prefer, you can pour
the remaining dressing into a
small bowl and serve it at the
table for drizzling (instead of
mixing it through the freekeh).

udon miso soup
with crispy glazed salmon

4 x 100g (3½ oz) salmon fillets, skin on
1 small eggplant (aubergine) (230g/8 oz),
  sliced into 1cm (½ in) rounds
2 tablespoons mirin (Japanese rice wine)
2 tablespoons soy sauce
2 teaspoons hot chilli sauce
3 cups (45g/1½ oz) trimmed watercress sprigs
seaweed sprinkle (see *recipe*, page 232), to serve
miso noodle broth
2 tablespoons white miso paste (shiro)
2 tablespoons soy sauce
2 tablespoons mirin (Japanese rice wine)
1 tablespoon finely grated ginger
1.5 litres (50 fl oz) water
220g (7¾ oz) dried udon noodles

To make the miso noodle broth, place the miso paste,
soy sauce, mirin and ginger in a large saucepan. Add
1 cup (250ml/8½ fl oz) of the water to the pan and whisk
until smooth and the miso is dissolved. Add the remaining
1.25 litres (42¼ fl oz) of water to the pan and bring to
the boil over high heat. Add the noodles and cook for
8 minutes or until tender.

   While the miso noodle broth is cooking, heat a large
non-stick frying pan over high heat. Add the salmon,
skin-side down, and cook for 3 minutes or until the skin
is crisp. Turn and cook for a further 1 minute. Remove
from the pan and keep warm.

   Place the eggplant in the pan and cook for 3 minutes
each side or until golden. While the eggplant is cooking,
place the mirin, soy and chilli sauce in a medium jug and
whisk to combine. Add the sauce mixture to the pan
with the eggplant and cook for a further 1 minute or
until the sauce reduces to a syrupy glaze.

   Divide the noodles between serving bowls and ladle
the miso broth over. Top with the salmon and eggplant
and drizzle with the glaze. Serve with the watercress
and seaweed sprinkle. **SERVES 4**

cook's note
It's easy to get creative with
this flavourful Asian broth.
You can swap the salmon
for thick slices of firm tofu
– simply cook it in the pan
for 3 minutes each side or
until golden. If you prefer
chicken, add 2 breast fillets
to the pan and cook for
4–5 minutes each side or
until tender and cooked
through. Slice to serve.

simple red curry sweet potato soup

1 tablespoon extra virgin olive oil
1 onion, finely chopped
⅓ cup (100g/3½ oz) store-bought red curry paste
1 tablespoon finely grated ginger
1kg (2 lb 3 oz) orange sweet potato (kumara),
   peeled and grated
1 litre good-quality vegetable stock
1 cup (250ml/8½ fl oz) coconut cream
sea salt flakes, for sprinkling
shredded green onions (scallions), to serve
micro (baby) coriander (cilantro) leaves, to serve
lime wedges, to serve

Place a large saucepan over medium-high heat. Add
the oil and onion and cook for 3 minutes or until soft.
Add the curry paste and cook for 1 minute or until
fragrant. Add the ginger, sweet potato, stock and
coconut cream and bring to a simmer. Cover with
a tight-fitting lid and cook for 8–10 minutes or until
the sweet potato is soft.

   Sprinkle with salt to taste and ladle into serving
bowls. Top with onion and coriander and serve with
lime wedges. SERVES 4

cook's note
This easy soup is what I call
comfort in a bowl. Whether it's
a cold day, I need a nourishing
boost or I'm just in the mood
for something warming and
fragrant, it's fast, fresh and it
makes me feel good!

char-grilled fennel, freekeh and labne salad

4 bulbs baby fennel (520g/1 lb 2 oz), trimmed
   and halved
480g (1 lb) cavolo nero (Tuscan kale) (about 8 stalks),
   stems removed
extra virgin olive oil, for brushing
2½ cups (400g/14 oz) cooked freekeh
1 cup (24g/¾ oz) flat-leaf parsley leaves
⅓ cup (130g/4½ oz) dried cranberries or raisins
½ cup (80g/2¾ oz) almonds, toasted
   and roughly chopped
¼ cup (60ml/2 fl oz) pomegranate molasses
   or caramelised balsamic vinegar
sea salt flakes, for sprinkling
labne, to serve
extra virgin olive oil, extra, to serve

Heat a char-grill pan or barbecue over medium-high heat. Brush the fennel and cavolo nero lightly with oil. Cook the fennel for 4–5 minutes each side or until charred and slightly softened. Set aside and keep warm. Cook the cavolo nero for 1 minute each side or until crisp.

Place the freekeh, parsley, cranberries, almonds and pomegranate molasses in a large bowl and toss to combine.

Divide the freekeh salad, fennel and cavolo nero between serving bowls. Sprinkle with salt and top with labne and a little extra oil to serve. **SERVES 4**

cook's notes

One of the easiest meals to create, this grain salad takes minimal prep but is bursting with sweet-savoury goodness.

You can swap feta for the labne if you like, and your favourite cooked grain (like brown rice or burghul) for the freekeh.

pummelled kale with golden cauliflower and haloumi croutons

2kg (4 lb 7 oz) cauliflower (about 2 large heads),
   trimmed and cut into florets
⅓ cup (80ml/2¾ fl oz) extra virgin olive oil
250g (8¾ oz) haloumi, chopped
8 sprigs marjoram
⅓ cup (45g/1½ oz) slivered almonds, toasted
pummelled kale salad
500g (1 lb 2 oz) kale (about 10 stalks), stems
   removed and leaves torn into small pieces
2 tablespoons extra virgin olive oil
¼ cup (40g/1½ oz) currants
1 teaspoon finely grated lemon rind
¼ cup (60ml/2 fl oz) lemon juice

Preheat oven to 220°C (425°F). Line 2 baking trays
with non-stick baking paper.

Place the cauliflower florets in a large bowl and
add ¼ cup (60ml/2 fl oz) of the oil. Toss to coat and
divide between the trays. Roast for 20 minutes.

Place the haloumi and marjoram in the bowl and
top with the remaining 1 tablespoon of oil. Toss to
coat, arrange over the cauliflower on the trays and
roast for a further 20 minutes or until the haloumi
and cauliflower are golden.

While the cauliflower and haloumi are roasting,
make the pummelled kale salad. Place the kale, oil,
currants, lemon rind and juice in a large bowl. Toss to
combine and, using your hands, rub the dressing into
the kale for 8 minutes or until the kale is softened.

Divide the kale salad between serving bowls and
top with the warm cauliflower and haloumi. Sprinkle
with the almonds and serve immediately. **SERVES 4**

cook's note
I seriously laughed when
I heard about massaging kale
in its dressing. Then I tried it
and I was truly sold. It's the
best way to eat raw kale. I still
can't (with a straight face) write
'massage the kale' so, coming
from a houseful of energetic
boys, I've called it pummelled
kale instead – you get the idea!

roasted carrot and turmeric soup

¼ cup (60ml/2 fl oz) extra virgin olive oil
2 teaspoons ground turmeric
2 teaspoons ground cumin
sea salt and cracked black pepper
6 carrots, peeled and quartered lengthways
1 onion, peeled and cut into wedges
2 litres (68 fl oz) good-quality vegetable stock
¼ cup (70g/2½ oz) hulled tahini
1 x 400g (14 oz) can chickpeas (garbanzo beans),
   drained, rinsed and lightly crushed
¼ cup (3g/¼ oz) coriander (cilantro) leaves
plain Greek-style (thick) yoghurt, to serve
hulled tahini, extra, to serve

Preheat oven to 220°C (425°F). Line 2 large baking
trays with non-stick baking paper.

Place the oil, turmeric, cumin, salt and pepper in a
large bowl and mix to combine. Add the carrot and
onion and toss to combine. Divide between the 2 trays
and roast for 25 minutes or until golden and just tender.

Transfer the roasted vegetables to a large saucepan.
Add the stock and tahini and, using a hand-held stick
blender, blend until smooth.

Place the soup over medium heat and bring to a
simmer. Add the chickpeas and cook for a further
5 minutes or until the soup is hot.

Divide between serving bowls and sprinkle with the
coriander. Top with a swirl of yoghurt and a swirl of
extra tahini to serve. **SERVES 4**

cook's note
This is such a great soup
to make big batches of and
freeze for lunches or speedy
dinners. Pour the cooled
soup into airtight containers
(without the coriander,
yoghurt and extra tahini)
and place in the freezer.
Thaw and reheat as you
need it, adding the garnishes
when you're ready to serve.

mushroom fried rice with crispy chilli eggs

2 tablespoons extra virgin olive oil
1 tablespoon finely grated ginger
1 long red chilli, seeds removed and sliced
400g (14 oz) mixed sliced and small whole mushrooms
4 cups (800g/1 lb 12 oz) cooked brown rice
⅓ cup (80ml/2¾ fl oz) Chinese cooking wine (Shaoxing)
2 tablespoons soy sauce
4 green onions (scallions), sliced
sliced long red chilli, extra, to serve
kecap manis (sweet soy sauce), to serve
crispy chilli eggs
2 teaspoons sesame oil
2 tablespoons extra virgin olive oil
1 long red chilli, finely chopped
2 green onions (scallions), finely chopped
4 eggs

Heat the oil in a large deep-sided frying pan over medium heat. Add the ginger and chilli and cook for 1 minute. Add the mushrooms and cook, stirring occasionally, for 15–20 minutes or until golden (see *cook's note*). Add the rice and cook for a further 4 minutes or until heated through. Add the cooking wine and soy sauce and cook, stirring, for 3 minutes. Set aside and keep warm.

To make the crispy chilli eggs, heat the sesame oil and olive oil in a large non-stick frying pan over high heat. Add the chilli and onion and cook, stirring, for 1 minute or until the onion is light golden in colour. Crack the eggs into the hot oil mixture in the pan and cook, spooning a little oil over the tops, for 2–3 minutes or until the eggwhites are set and the edges are crisp.

Divide the fried rice between serving bowls and top with the eggs and any extra oil. Sprinkle with the onion and serve with extra chilli and kecap manis. **SERVES 4**

cook's note
Don't be afraid to brown the mushrooms for long enough that they've dried out a little bit. They should be golden and slightly crisp on the edges, not mushy and soft. Trust me, it's worth the wait – you'll get really delicious flavour and texture!

CHAPTER THREE

fields
of
green

ne day last year, *coffee-in-hand* at home, I was overlooking my lovely (if a little small) AREA OF LAWN, when the thought struck me – why am I *growing grass*?! I've always had HERBS IN POTS on my windowsill, but never thought I had space for much more. What if my *mini oasis* of lawn could become a different KIND OF GREEN? A pep-talk from my local grower friends ensued, and with that I had the confidence to replace some turf with a *modest patch* of ORGANIC VEGETABLES. My new *field of greens* is now my happy place. Who would've thought I'd become a GARDEN GIRL! It just shows, even if you have a teeny outdoor space, it's amazing what you can produce.

oven-baked super-green falafels

1 x 400g (14 oz) can chickpeas (garbanzo beans),
    drained and rinsed
1 onion, finely chopped
1 cup (120g/4¼ oz) frozen peas, slightly thawed
2 tablespoons white chia seeds
1 cup (90g/3 oz) finely chopped broccoli
2 cups (70g/2½ oz) firmly packed shredded
    kale leaves
1 cup (24g/¾ oz) flat-leaf parsley leaves
½ cup (8g/¼ oz) mint leaves
1½ teaspoons ground cumin
½ teaspoon baking powder
sea salt and cracked black pepper
extra virgin olive oil, for brushing
flatbreads, to serve (see *cook's notes*)
rocket (arugula), to serve
sliced radishes, to serve
labne, to serve

Preheat oven to 220°C (425°F). Line a large baking tray
with non-stick baking paper.
   Place the chickpeas, onion, peas, chia seeds, broccoli,
kale, parsley, mint, cumin, baking powder, salt and
pepper in a food processor and process until very
finely chopped.
   Press 2-tablespoon portions of the mixture into
patties and place on the tray. Brush the patties
generously with oil and bake for 15 minutes. Brush the
patties with more oil and bake for a further 15 minutes
or until golden and crisp.
   Divide flatbreads between serving plates and top with
rocket, radish, labne and the falafels to serve. **MAKES 16**

cook's notes

I used charcoal flatbreads, not
just for taste – they also look
so striking against the fresh
colours of the vegetables. You
can use any type of flatbread
you wish, from seeded to
Lebanese to wholemeal – the
choice is yours!

Keep any leftover or extra
falafels in an airtight container
in the fridge for up to 2 days.
They make a great on-the-go
snack and will add a little more
substance to your work salad.

roasted baby beet and freekeh salad

12 baby beetroot (300g/10½ oz), trimmed
and halved (see *cook's notes*)
¼ cup (60ml/2 fl oz) extra virgin olive oil
sea salt and cracked black pepper
100g (3½ oz) beetroot leaves
3½ cups (560g/1 lb 4 oz) cooked freekeh
½ cup (90g/3 oz) pomegranate seeds
2 tablespoons chopped tarragon leaves
¾ cup (18g/½ oz) flat-leaf parsley leaves
¾ cup (12g/½ oz) mint leaves
150g (5¼ oz) soft feta
¼ cup (35g/1¼ oz) pistachios, chopped
zesty pomegranate dressing
2 tablespoons pomegranate molasses
or balsamic glaze
1 tablespoon orange juice
finely grated zest of half an orange
sea salt flakes, for sprinkling

Preheat oven to 200°C (400°F). Line 2 large baking trays
with non-stick baking paper.

Place the beetroot in a large bowl, add 1½ tablespoons
of the oil and sprinkle with salt. Toss to coat and spread
over 1 of the trays. Roast for 20 minutes or until tender.

Reduce the oven temperature to 180°C (350°F). Place
the beetroot leaves on the remaining tray and drizzle
with the remaining 1½ tablespoons of oil. Sprinkle with
salt and roast for 12 minutes or until golden.

While the beetroot is roasting, make the zesty
pomegranate dressing. Place the pomegranate molasses,
orange juice, orange zest and salt in a small bowl and mix
to combine.

Place the freekeh, pomegranate seeds, tarragon,
parsley and mint in a large bowl. Add the beetroot and
toss to combine. Divide the salad between serving bowls
and top with the feta, beetroot leaves, pistachios and
the dressing. Sprinkle with pepper to serve. **SERVES 4**

cook's notes

If you can, buy the baby beets
in bunches, with the leaves
intact and in good shape.
That way, you can trim the
leaves from the beets and use
both elements in this salad.

I love the nutty taste of freekeh
for this recipe, but you can
absolutely get creative with the
base – brown rice works well,
as does quinoa, pearl barley
or even lentils.

90

my favourite char-grilled broccoli salad

1kg (2 lb 3 oz) broccoli (about 3 heads), thickly sliced
extra virgin olive oil, for brushing
sea salt and cracked black pepper
2 cups (50g/1¾ oz) mixed red-veined sorrel and baby
   rocket (arugula) leaves
175g (6 oz) marinated feta
1 x quantity honey seed sprinkle (see *recipe*, page 232)
1 x quantity green dressing (see *recipe*, page 228)

Heat a char-grill pan or barbecue over medium-high heat.
Lightly brush both sides of the broccoli with oil and
sprinkle with salt and pepper. Cook for 4–5 minutes
each side or until tender and slightly charred.

   Divide the broccoli and mixed leaves between serving
bowls. Crumble the feta and honey seed sprinkle over the
salads and top with the green dressing to serve. SERVES 4

cook's notes
This salad is high on my
rotation list of late. In the
same way it does meat,
char-grilling adds such a
great flavour to the broccoli.

You can always switch out
the broccoli for thick slices
of cauliflower. And while you
have the barbecue on, why
not add any other vegetables
that you'd usually grill – like
sliced zucchini (courgette),
orange sweet potato (kumara)
or even sweet corn on the cob.

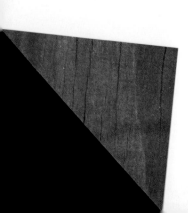

cucumber rolls
with crispy chia salmon

3–4 large telegraph cucumbers
2 cups (50g/1¾ oz) baby mustard greens or
   rocket (arugula)
1 x quantity edamame avo smash (see *recipe*, page 230)
1 x quantity pickled beetroot (see *recipe*, page 226)
lime halves, to serve
crispy chia salmon
½ cup (50g/1¾ oz) quinoa flakes
½ cup (60g/2 oz) almond meal (ground almonds)
¼ cup (50g/1¾ oz) chia seeds
sea salt and cracked black pepper
2 eggwhites
extra virgin olive oil, for cooking
4 x 100g (3½ oz) skinless salmon fillets

To make the crispy chia salmon, place the quinoa flakes, almond meal, chia seeds, salt and pepper in a large shallow bowl and mix to combine. Place the eggwhites in a medium bowl and whisk until fluffy. Heat a little oil in a medium non-stick frying pan over medium heat. Working in batches, dip the salmon into the eggwhite, then press both sides into the chia mixture to coat. Cook for 2–3 minutes each side or until golden. Cut into large pieces and set aside.

Slice the cucumber into long thin strips using a mandolin or vegetable peeler. Arrange 6–8 overlapping strips on a serving plate. Top with one-quarter of the mustard greens, edamame avo smash, pickled beetroot and salmon. Roll the cucumber to enclose. Repeat with the remaining ingredients to make a total of 4 rolls. Squeeze lime juice over the rolls to serve. **MAKES 4**

cook's notes

The long cucumber strips make a great wrapper for so many things. I tend to use them as you would nori or flatbreads. A mandolin makes light work of cutting the thin slices.

You can swap the salmon in this recipe for any firm fish fillet of your choice, or even pieces of chicken breast fillet if you prefer. Just ensure the chicken has enough time in the pan to cook through.

miso brown rice and broccoli balls

1 cup (240g/8½ oz) fresh ricotta
2 tablespoons white miso paste (shiro)
1 tablespoon finely grated ginger
2 cups (400g/14 oz) cooked brown rice
2 cups (200g/7 oz) finely chopped broccoli
2 green onions (scallions), thinly sliced
sea salt flakes
¾ cup (100g/3½ oz) sesame seeds
extra virgin olive oil, for brushing
miso carrot salad
1 tablespoon white miso paste (shiro)
2 tablespoons mirin (Japanese rice wine)
1 tablespoon honey
300g (10½ oz) heirloom Dutch carrots, scrubbed,
   trimmed and quartered lengthways
2 cups (50g/1¾ oz) red-veined sorrel or baby
   spinach leaves

Preheat oven to 200°C (400°F). Line a large baking tray with non-stick baking paper.

Place the ricotta, miso paste and ginger in a large bowl and mix to combine. Add the rice, broccoli, onion and salt and mix to combine.

Place the sesame seeds on a small plate. Shape ¼-cup portions of the broccoli mixture into balls and roll in the sesame to coat. Place on the tray and brush generously with oil. Bake for 25 minutes or until golden.

While the broccoli balls are baking, make the miso carrot salad. Place the miso paste, mirin and honey in a large bowl and mix to combine. Add the carrot and red-veined sorrel and toss to combine.

Divide the salad between serving bowls and top with the broccoli balls to serve. **SERVES 4**

cook's notes
It's really easy to bake trays and trays of these rice balls and freeze them for later.

You can swap the rice for quinoa or other cooked grains.

rainbow chard rolls

3 cups (480g/1 lb) cooked quinoa
3 cups (240g/8½ oz) grated beetroot
¾ cup (120g/4¼ oz) pepitas (pumpkin seeds),
   toasted and roughly chopped
1 cup (24g/¾ oz) flat-leaf parsley leaves, chopped
2 teaspoons finely grated lemon rind
sea salt and cracked black pepper
275g (10 oz) firm goat's cheese, crumbled
12–15 medium stalks rainbow chard or silverbeet
   (Swiss chard), stems and spines trimmed
400g (14 oz) vine-ripened cherry tomatoes
1 tablespoon extra virgin olive oil
1 x quantity creamy cashew sauce
   (see *recipe*, page 228)

Preheat oven to 180°C (350°F). Line 2 baking trays with
non-stick baking paper.

Place the quinoa, beetroot, pepitas, parsley, lemon
rind, salt and pepper in a large bowl and mix to combine.
Sprinkle with the goat's cheese and fold to combine.

Place the chard leaves in a large heatproof bowl and
cover with boiling water. Allow to stand for 1 minute or
until just softened. Drain and pat dry with absorbent
kitchen paper.

Place ¼-cup portions of the quinoa mixture onto each
leaf, tuck in the sides of the leaf and roll to enclose the
filling. Place the rolls on 1 of the trays and roast for
15 minutes.

Place the tomatoes on the remaining tray, drizzle with
oil and sprinkle with salt and pepper. Add to the oven
and roast for 10–15 minutes or until blistered.

Divide the rolls and tomatoes between serving plates
and serve with the creamy cashew sauce. **SERVES 4**

cook's note

This is one of those recipes
that I like to play around with.
You can swap the quinoa for
cooked brown or black rice,
swap the grated beetroot for
carrot. The options are only
limited by the seasons and
your imagination!

miso cabbage japanese pancakes

5 eggwhites
¼ cup (40g/1½ oz) brown rice flour
2 tablespoons white miso paste (shiro)
2 tablespoons finely grated ginger
3 cups (150g/5¼ oz) finely shredded kale leaves
4 cups (320g/11¼ oz) finely shredded
   Chinese cabbage
4 green onions (scallions), thinly sliced
extra virgin olive oil, for cooking
shichimi togarashi or chilli flakes,
   to serve (optional)
pickled ginger and carrot salad
100g (3½ oz) store-bought pickled ginger,
   pickling liquid reserved
3 carrots, peeled and shredded using
   a julienne or vegetable peeler
4 green onions (scallions), thinly sliced

Place the eggwhites, flour, miso paste and ginger in a large bowl and whisk to combine. Add the kale, cabbage and onion and mix to combine. Allow to stand for 5 minutes.

Heat a little oil in a medium non-stick frying pan over medium-low heat. Add 1 cup of the cabbage mixture to the pan and press to flatten. Cook for 8 minutes each side or until golden and crisp. Set aside and keep warm. Repeat with the remaining mixture, adding more oil as necessary.

To make the pickled ginger and carrot salad, place the ginger, pickling liquid, carrot and onion in a large bowl and toss to combine.

Divide the crispy pancakes between serving plates and top with the carrot salad. Sprinkle with togarashi to serve. MAKES 4

cook's note
The eggwhite in these pancakes is a great protein hit, but if you want to add something extra, feel free. Try topping each plate with a few very thin slices of rare-roasted beef, shredded cooked chicken, some crispy fried tofu or some pan-fried firm white fish (such as cod).

ating *your greens* doesn't have to be all STEAMED SIDES and *snoozy salads*. Trust me, once YOU'RE INSPIRED you'll want to weave more into your *everyday cooking*. There are so many TEXTURES AND FLAVOURS to play with.

simple vegetable hash browns

1 x 400g (14 oz) can red kidney beans,
   drained and rinsed
4 cups (480g/1 lb) grated carrot, beetroot, pumpkin
   or orange sweet potato (kumara) (see *cook's note*)
1 cup (50g/1¾ oz) finely shredded kale leaves
1 cup (16g/½ oz) mint leaves, chopped
1 cup (24g/¾ oz) flat-leaf parsley leaves, chopped
⅓ cup (90g/3 oz) hulled tahini
¼ cup (50g/1¾ oz) chia seeds
sea salt and cracked black pepper
extra virgin olive oil, for drizzling
1 cup (280g/10 oz) plain Greek-style (thick) yoghurt
1 clove garlic, crushed
2 cucumbers, thinly sliced

Preheat oven grill (broiler) to high. Line a large baking
tray with non-stick baking paper.

Place the beans in a large bowl and mash with a
fork into a rough paste. Add the carrot, kale, half the
mint, half the parsley, the tahini, chia, salt and pepper
and mix to combine.

Shape ¼-cup portions of the vegetable mixture into
8cm (3 in) patties and place on the tray. Drizzle with oil
and grill for 15 minutes or until golden and crisp.

Place the yoghurt and garlic in a small bowl and mix
to combine. Serve the hash browns with the cucumber,
the remaining mint and parsley and the garlic yoghurt.
MAKES 14

cook's note
I've mixed 1 cup of each
vegetable option in these
hash browns, for a boost of
flavour, colour and nutrients.
You can mix and match
your favourite combination
or just stick with one type
of veg – either way it's yum!

charred cabbage and warm apple salad

1 small green cabbage (800g/1 lb 12 oz), trimmed
    and quartered
¼ cup (60ml/2 fl oz) extra virgin olive oil
sea salt flakes, for sprinkling
labne, to serve
mixed salad greens, to serve
warm apple salad
¼ cup (60ml/2 fl oz) extra virgin olive oil
12 sage leaves
⅓ cup (35g/1¼ oz) walnuts, roughly chopped
⅓ cup (80ml/2¾ fl oz) apple cider vinegar
1 tablespoon honey
2 Granny Smith (green) apples, thinly sliced
    into rounds

Place the cabbage on a tray, drizzle with the oil and
sprinkle with salt. Heat a large non-stick frying pan
over medium-high heat. Cook the cabbage on each
cut side for 8–10 minutes or until well charred and
tender. Set aside and keep warm.

   To make the warm apple salad, wipe out the frying
pan and return it to medium-high heat. Add the oil,
sage and walnuts and cook, stirring, for 3–4 minutes
or until lightly golden. Remove the pan from the heat,
add the vinegar and honey and stir to combine. Add
the apple and gently toss to coat.

   Divide the cabbage and the apple salad between
serving plates, spooning any extra dressing over
the top. Serve with labne and salad greens. **SERVES 4**

cook's note
I know it looks a bit strange
to see the cabbage so charred
and black, but trust me – it's
absolutely delicious. It's one
of those things I discovered
and wished I'd found sooner!
To get an even charring of the
cabbage, press the wedges
firmly into the pan so that the
surface makes complete
contact with the heat.

zucchini pies

6 x 180g (6¼ oz) zucchinis (courgettes)
extra virgin olive oil, for brushing
1 cup (200g/7 oz) cottage cheese
1 cup (240g/8½ oz) fresh ricotta
180g (6¼ oz) English spinach, stems trimmed,
   leaves blanched and chopped
2 eggs
2 teaspoons finely grated lemon rind
2 tablespoons chopped dill sprigs
2 tablespoons chopped flat-leaf parsley leaves
sea salt and cracked black pepper

Preheat oven to 160°C (325°F). Lightly grease
4 x 1½-cup-capacity (375ml/12½ fl oz) rectangular
pie tins.

   Thinly slice the zucchinis lengthways using a mandolin
or vegetable peeler. Position the zucchini slices around
the edges of the tins (the centre of each slice should
sit on the rim of the tins). Allow the tips of the zucchini
to overlap slightly to line the base of the tins, and let the
opposite ends overhang the edges, ready to fold in later.

   Place the cottage cheese, ricotta, spinach, eggs, lemon
rind, dill, parsley, salt and pepper in a large bowl and mix
to combine. Divide the filling between the pie dishes.
Fold in the overhanging zucchini to enclose the filling
and brush the tops of the pies with a little oil.

   Bake for 30–35 minutes or until the zucchini is just
golden and the filling is set. **SERVES 4**

cook's note
I love this fresh take on
traditional spinach and
cheese pies – they're simple
to make and are just as tasty
warm from the oven as they
are cold. Serve with your
favourite relish or a spoonful
of tzatziki.

charred roasted broccoli and haloumi

650g (1 lb 7 oz) broccoli (about 2 heads), thickly sliced
350g (12¼ oz) haloumi, thickly sliced
studio topping
¼ cup (50g/1¾ oz) capers
2 onions, thinly sliced
2 long red chillies, seeds removed and sliced
2 tablespoons finely shredded lemon rind
8 small sprigs oregano
¼ cup (60ml/2 fl oz) extra virgin olive oil
rocket (arugula) leaves and lemon cheeks, to serve

Preheat oven grill (broiler) to high. Line a large baking tray with non-stick baking paper.

To make the studio topping, place the capers, onion, chilli, lemon rind, oregano and oil in a medium bowl and mix to combine.

Place the broccoli and haloumi on the tray and spoon the studio topping over to roughly coat. Place the tray on a middle shelf in the oven and grill for 20–25 minutes or until the broccoli, haloumi and onion are charred and golden.

Serve with rocket leaves and top with a generous squeeze of lemon juice to serve. **SERVES 2**

cook's note
This dish serves 2 people as a main, but if you want to add it to the table with some roasted meat or grilled fish, it makes a really great vegetable side that serves 4 people.

spinach, tahini and almond pasta

350g (12¼ oz) dried wholemeal (whole-wheat) pasta
200g (7 oz) English spinach, stems trimmed
chopped roasted almonds, to serve
tahini sauce
½ cup (140g/5 oz) hulled tahini
⅔ cup (160ml/5½ fl oz) water
2 tablespoons lemon juice
1 clove garlic, crushed
⅓ cup (5g/¼ oz) mint leaves, chopped
2 tablespoons chopped dill sprigs
⅓ cup (8g/¼ oz) flat-leaf parsley leaves, chopped
sea salt and cracked black pepper

To make the tahini sauce, place the tahini, water, lemon juice, garlic, mint, dill, parsley, salt and pepper in a food processor or blender and process until smooth.

Cook the pasta in a large saucepan of salted boiling water for 8–10 minutes or until al dente. Drain, reserving ½ cup (125ml/4¼ fl oz) of the cooking water, and return the pasta to the pan. Add the spinach and stir until wilted. Add the tahini sauce and toss to combine, with a little of the reserved pasta water if the sauce needs thinning.

Divide the pasta between serving bowls and top with the almonds to serve. **SERVES 4**

cook's note
This clever tahini sauce lends the pasta a velvety finish, without the need for cream. Sprinkle with parmesan and pepper to finish, if you like.

quinoa tabouli with seared feta and lemon tahini dressing

4 cups (640g/1 lb 7 oz) cooked red or white quinoa
300g (10½ oz) cherry tomatoes, halved
2 cucumbers, thinly sliced
1½ cups (36g/1¼ oz) small flat-leaf parsley leaves
1 cup (16g/½ oz) mint leaves, torn
4 green onions (scallions), thinly sliced
2 tablespoons extra virgin olive oil
sea salt and cracked black pepper
400g (14 oz) firm feta, cut into 4 thick slices
extra virgin olive oil, for brushing
lemon tahini dressing
½ cup (140g/5 oz) hulled tahini
⅔ cup (160ml/5½ fl oz) lemon juice
1 clove garlic, crushed
⅓ cup (80ml/2¾ fl oz) water
sea salt flakes

Place the quinoa, tomatoes, cucumber, parsley, mint, onion, oil, salt and pepper in a large bowl and gently toss to combine.

To make the lemon tahini dressing, place the tahini, lemon juice, garlic, water and salt in a small bowl. Whisk until smooth and set aside.

Preheat oven grill (broiler) to medium-high. Line a baking tray with non-stick baking paper. Brush the feta with a little oil and place on the tray. Grill for 4–6 minutes or until golden.

Divide the quinoa tabouli between serving plates and top with the feta. Drizzle with the lemon tahini dressing to serve. **SERVES 4**

cook's note
This tabouli is my favourite creation when I have leftover cooked grains in the fridge from the night before. You can really use any base you like – burghul, pearl barley, freekeh or brown rice will all work well.

easy green egg and parmesan bakes

250g (8¾ oz) frozen spinach, thawed
2½ cups (625ml/21 fl oz) milk
5 eggs
¾ cup (60g/2 oz) finely grated parmesan
sea salt and cracked black pepper
4 x 1.5cm-thick (½ in) slices wholemeal (whole-wheat)
  bread (250g/8¾ oz)
3 cups (300g/10½ oz) finely chopped broccoli
⅓ cup (90g/3 oz) store-bought pesto
finely grated parmesan, extra, for sprinkling

Preheat oven to 180°C (350°F). Lightly grease
4 x 1½-cup-capacity (375ml/12½ fl oz) ovenproof dishes.
   Place the spinach in a sieve and press to remove
the excess water. Place between sheets of absorbent
kitchen paper and squeeze to remove any remaining
moisture. Roughly chop and set aside.
   Place the milk, eggs, parmesan, salt and pepper in
a large bowl and whisk to combine. Tear the bread
into large chunks and add to the egg mixture. Toss to
coat. Add the spinach, broccoli and pesto and fold to
combine. Allow to stand for 10 minutes.
   Divide the mixture evenly between the dishes
and sprinkle with a little extra parmesan. Bake for
25–30 minutes or until the egg is just set. Sprinkle
with extra parmesan to serve. **SERVES 4**

cook's note
You can make one large
version of this if you prefer.
You'll need a lightly greased
2-litre-capacity (68 fl oz)
ovenproof dish. Just increase
the baking time to 45 minutes
so it cooks all the way through.

CHAPTER FOUR

out

of

time

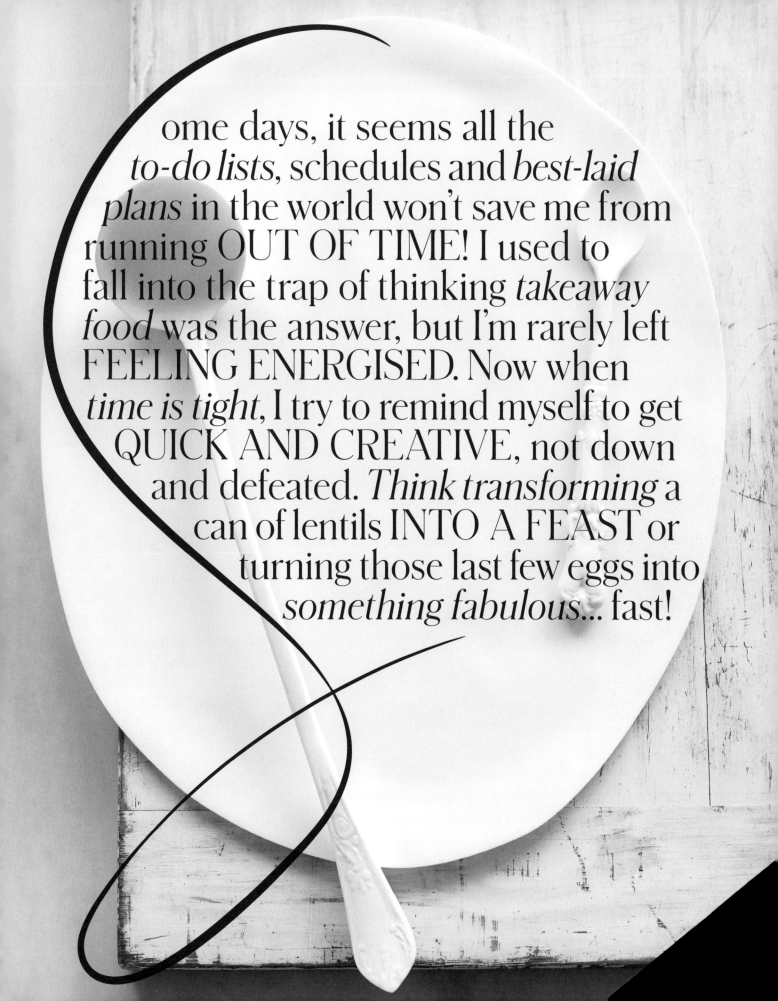

ome days, it seems all the to-do lists, schedules and *best-laid plans* in the world won't save me from running OUT OF TIME! I used to fall into the trap of thinking *takeaway food* was the answer, but I'm rarely left FEELING ENERGISED. Now when *time is tight,* I try to remind myself to get QUICK AND CREATIVE, not down and defeated. *Think transforming* a can of lentils INTO A FEAST or turning those last few eggs into *something fabulous...* fast!

spaghetti with super-green almond pesto

350g (12¼ oz) dried wholemeal (whole-wheat) pasta
2 tablespoons extra virgin olive oil
4 cloves garlic, sliced
1 tablespoon finely grated lemon rind
½ cup (80g/2¾ oz) almonds, roughly chopped
900g (2 lb) cavolo nero (Tuscan kale) (about 15 stalks),
   stems removed and leaves roughly chopped
sea salt and cracked black pepper
extra virgin olive oil, extra, for drizzling
150g (5¼ oz) goat's cheese, sliced
roughly chopped almonds, extra, to serve (optional)

Cook the pasta in a large saucepan of salted boiling
water for 8–10 minutes or until al dente.
  Drain the pasta, reserving ½ cup (125ml/4¼ fl oz) of
the cooking water. Set the pasta and reserved water
aside and return the pan to medium heat. Add the oil,
garlic, lemon rind and almonds and cook, stirring, for
3 minutes or until the garlic is soft and the almonds
are just golden. Add the cavolo nero, salt and pepper
and cook, stirring, for 4 minutes or until just wilted.
Return the pasta and reserved water to the pan and
toss to coat.
  Divide the pasta between serving plates. Drizzle
with extra oil and top with the goat's cheese. Sprinkle
with pepper and extra almonds to serve. **SERVES 4**

cook's notes

If you like, you can swap out
cavolo nero for its super-green
cousin, kale – you'll only need
about 6 stalks, stems removed
and leaves chopped.

To add extra richness and
flavour to this pasta, top each
plate with a soft-poached egg.

If you're feeling fishy, you
could always add 90g (3 oz)
flaked hot-smoked trout to
each serving.

mint, pea, spinach and chia fritters

1 cup (120g/4¼ oz) frozen peas, thawed
250g (8¾ oz) frozen spinach, thawed
½ cup (8g/¼ oz) mint leaves, chopped
¼ cup (6g/¼ oz) dill sprigs, chopped
1 cup (240g/8½ oz) fresh ricotta
2 eggs
¼ cup (50g/1¾ oz) chia seeds
sea salt and cracked black pepper
extra virgin olive oil, for cooking
lemon cheeks, to serve
rocket (arugula), to serve
store-bought tzatziki, to serve
shredded mint leaves, extra, to serve

Place the peas in a large bowl, crush with a fork until partially mashed and set aside.

Place the spinach in a sieve and press to remove the excess water. Place between sheets of absorbent kitchen paper and squeeze to remove any remaining moisture. Roughly chop the spinach, add to the peas and mix to combine.

Add the mint, dill, ricotta, eggs, chia seeds, salt and pepper to the pea mixture and mix to combine. Allow to stand for 10 minutes.

Heat a large non-stick frying pan over medium-high heat. Add a little oil to the pan. Using wet hands, shape ¼-cup portions of the mixture into patties. Cook, in batches, for 3 minutes each side or until golden brown, adding more oil to the pan as necessary. Remove the fritters from the pan and keep warm.

Divide the fritters between serving plates with the lemon cheeks, rocket and tzatziki. Sprinkle with extra mint to serve. **MAKES 8**

cook's notes
I always make a few more of these clean green fritters than I need – just wrap and keep them in the fridge for 1–2 days – they're the best for school lunchboxes or to add to your work salad.

These fritters are also great for party nibbles. Cook 1-tablespoon portions of the mixture and top them with a small spoonful of tzatziki. If you like, add a little smoked salmon to serve.

simple vegetable sushi

8 sheets toasted nori
125g (4½ oz) baby spinach leaves
3 cucumbers, halved and sliced lengthways
**3 carrots, peeled and grated or shredded using
 a julienne peeler**
2 avocados, thickly sliced
⅔ cup (10g/¼ oz) mint leaves
⅔ cup (60g/2 oz) store-bought pickled ginger
water, for brushing
soy sauce or coconut aminos, to serve
wasabi, to serve
store-bought pickled ginger, extra, to serve

Place 1 sheet of the nori, rough-side up, onto a clean surface. Arrange a line of overlapping spinach leaves to cover one-third of the sheet, leaving a 2cm (¾ in) border at the edge closest to you. Top the spinach with cucumber, carrot, avocado, mint and ginger.

Roll the nori to encase the filling, brushing the edge with a little water to seal the roll. Cut the roll in half. Repeat with the remaining nori sheets and fillings.

Serve the sushi rolls with soy, wasabi and extra ginger. **SERVES 4**

cook's note

You can choose to add all kinds of fillings to this sushi, so everyone will be happy and satisfied. Or if you have a few options on-hand, then each person can design their own combination! For each roll, you might like to add 2 slices smoked salmon, 45g (1½ oz) sashimi-grade salmon or tuna or 3 cooked and peeled prawns (shrimp). You could also try adding 45g (1½ oz) cooked shredded chicken or 3 very thin slices of roasted beef fillet per roll.

super-quick super-green soup

2 litres (68 fl oz) good-quality vegetable stock
2 cups (240g/8½ oz) frozen peas
900g (2 lb) broccoli (about 2 heads), roughly chopped
100g (3½ oz) English spinach leaves, roughly chopped
1 cup (120g/4¼ oz) almond meal (ground almonds)
1 tablespoon finely grated lemon rind
1 tablespoon lemon juice
½ cup (12g/½ oz) flat-leaf parsley leaves,
    roughly chopped
½ cup (8g/¼ oz) mint leaves, roughly chopped
sea salt and cracked black pepper
plain Greek-style (thick) yoghurt, to serve
sliced seeded nut bread (see *recipe*, page 234),
    to serve (optional)

Place the stock in a large saucepan over high heat and bring to the boil. Add the peas and broccoli and cook for 5 minutes or until just tender. Add the spinach, almond meal, lemon rind and juice, parsley, mint, salt and pepper and cook for 1 minute or until the spinach is wilted.

Using a hand-held stick blender, carefully blend the soup until smooth. Divide between serving bowls and top with yoghurt and pepper. Serve with bread. **SERVES 4**

cook's notes

This soup is my absolute stand-by saviour. I'll often make a large batch and freeze it in single portions to either take to the studio for lunch, or as a late-home nutritious dinner. It's such a warming feel-good meal.

I use almond meal to thicken the soup, and to add essential nutrients. To make this recipe nut-free, swap the almond meal for 1¼ cups (200g/7 oz) pepitas (pumpkin seeds) instead, blitzing them in a food processor until ground, or add 300g (10½ oz) drained silken tofu just before blending – delicious.

crispy mushroom tarts

1 small head garlic, halved crossways
4 sprigs tarragon
2 large flat mushrooms (200g/7 oz),
  stems trimmed (see *cook's notes*)
8 medium cup mushrooms (160g/5½ oz),
  stems removed (see *cook's notes*)
¼ cup (60ml/2 fl oz) extra virgin olive oil
sea salt and cracked black pepper
2 x 20cm (8 in) wholemeal (whole-wheat) tortillas
  or flatbreads
1 cup (240g/8½ oz) fresh ricotta
¾ cup (60g/2 oz) finely grated parmesan
radicchio or salad leaves, to serve

Preheat oven to 200°C (400°F). Line 2 baking trays
with non-stick baking paper.

Place the garlic, tarragon and mushrooms, stem-side
up, on 1 of the trays. Brush with 2 tablespoons of
the oil and sprinkle with salt and pepper. Roast for
20–25 minutes or until the mushrooms are tender.

While the mushrooms are roasting, place the tortillas
on the remaining tray, brushing each with ½ teaspoon
of the oil. Bake for 6 minutes or until just golden.

Place the ricotta and ½ cup (40g/1½ oz) of the
parmesan in a medium bowl. Sprinkle with salt and
pepper to taste and mix to combine. Spread the ricotta
mixture evenly over the tortillas and sprinkle with the
remaining ¼ cup (20g/¾ oz) of parmesan. Drizzle with
the remaining 1½ teaspoons of oil and bake for 5 minutes.

Arrange the mushrooms on the tart bases. Squeeze
the garlic from its skin onto the tarts and top with the
tarragon. Serve with salad leaves. **SERVES 2**

cook's notes

Feel free to use any
combination of mushrooms
and herbs that you like.

For a speedier option, forget
the mushrooms and use some
kale instead – there's no need
to pre-roast the kale. Just tear
up the leaves (stems removed)
and sprinkle onto the baked
ricotta tart base with the
remaining parmesan. Drizzle
with the oil, bake for 5 minutes
(longer for super-crispy kale)
and you're done!

zucchini noodles with lemon, ricotta and basil

4 large zucchinis (courgettes) (750g/1 lb 10 oz)
  (see *cook's notes*)
2 tablespoons extra virgin olive oil
3 cloves garlic, sliced
1 teaspoon cracked black pepper
1½ cups (360g/12½ oz) fresh ricotta
½ cup small basil leaves
2 teaspoons finely grated lemon rind
2 tablespoons lemon juice
sea salt flakes, for sprinkling
finely grated parmesan, to serve

Using a spiraliser or julienne peeler, cut the zucchinis into long thin noodles (zoodles) and set aside.

Heat a large non-stick frying pan over medium-high heat. Add the oil, garlic and pepper and cook for 2 minutes or until the garlic is soft.

Add the zucchini to the pan and toss to coat. Remove from the heat and divide the zucchini between serving bowls. Top with the ricotta, basil, lemon rind and juice. Sprinkle with salt and parmesan to serve. **SERVES 2**

cook's notes

If you're using a spiraliser, you'll need all 4 zucchinis (you lose the centre of the vegetable when spiralising). If you use a peeler instead, 3 zucchinis should be plenty.

I'll sometimes make this same recipe using wholemeal (whole-wheat) or regular spaghetti, cooked to al dente, in place of zoodles – you can even mix half-half!

toasted spiced lentil salad

2 onions, thinly sliced
2 x 400g (14 oz) cans lentils, rinsed and drained
¼ cup (60ml/2 fl oz) extra virgin olive oil
1 tablespoon ras el hanout (see *cook's notes*)
sea salt and cracked black pepper
4 cups (100g/3½ oz) baby spinach leaves
2 bulbs baby fennel, shaved lengthways
2 firm pears, thinly sliced
juice of half a lemon
extra virgin olive oil, extra, to serve
⅓ cup (50g/1¾ oz) shelled pistachios,
   roughly chopped

Preheat oven to 220°C (425°F). Line 2 baking trays
with non-stick baking paper.

Place the onion, lentils, oil, ras el hanout, salt and
pepper in a large bowl and toss to combine. Divide the
mixture between the trays and roast for 20 minutes
or until the onion and lentils are crisp.

While the lentils are roasting, place the spinach,
fennel, pear, lemon juice, salt and extra oil in a large
bowl and gently toss to combine.

Divide the lentils and salad between serving plates.
Drizzle with extra oil and sprinkle with the pistachios
to serve. **SERVES 4**

cook's notes
Ras el hanout is something
I always have on-hand in my
pantry – it's a North African
spice mix (read: great shortcut
to flavour) with up to 20 spices
in the one little jar! Think
cloves, cinnamon, cardamom,
chilli, coriander, paprika and
turmeric. Find it in spice shops
and greengrocers.

You can use canned chickpeas
(garbanzo beans) in place of
the lentils, if you prefer.

Crumble feta over this salad
for a flavour-boost finish.

fragrant lemongrass and coconut pumpkin

1 tablespoon shredded ginger
8 kaffir lime leaves, shredded
2 stalks lemongrass, white part only, bruised
  and halved lengthways
2 cups (500ml/17 fl oz) vegetable stock
2 cups (500ml/17 fl oz) coconut milk
1kg (2 lb 3 oz) pumpkin or orange sweet potato
  (kumara), peeled and chopped
200g (7 oz) snow peas (mange tout) or sugar snap peas
2 cups (50g/1¾ oz) baby spinach leaves
2 tablespoons lime juice
1 tablespoon fish sauce or coconut aminos
¾ cup (9g/¼ oz) coriander (cilantro) leaves
shredded kaffir lime leaves, extra, to serve
steamed brown rice, to serve (optional)

Place the ginger, lime leaves, lemongrass, stock and
coconut milk in a large deep-sided frying pan over
medium-high heat and bring to the boil. Add the
pumpkin, bring to a simmer and cook for 10 minutes
or until the pumpkin is tender.

Add the peas and spinach, stir to combine and cook
for 1 minute. Add the lime juice and fish sauce and stir
to combine. Divide between serving bowls and sprinkle
with the coriander and extra lime leaves. Serve with
rice. **SERVES 4**

cook's notes
It's super easy to add chicken
to this recipe – just chop
2 thigh fillets (400g/14 oz)
and add them to the pan with
the pumpkin, making sure
they're tender and cooked
through before serving.

If seafood is more your thing,
add 300g (10½ oz) chopped
firm white fish or salmon at
the same time as you add the
peas and spinach – cook for
an extra 1 minute.

green eggs in a pan

2 tablespoons extra virgin olive oil
1 onion, thinly sliced
1 tablespoon finely grated lemon rind
200g (7 oz) kale (about 4 stalks), stems removed
   and leaves shredded
150g (5¼ oz) baby spinach leaves
1 tablespoon lemon juice
sea salt and cracked black pepper
2 eggs
¼ cup (6g/¼ oz) dill sprigs
1 long red chilli, sliced
labne, to serve
sumac, for sprinkling
lemon wedges, to serve
wholemeal (whole-wheat) flatbreads,
   to serve (optional)

Preheat oven to 180°C (350°F). Place a large ovenproof
frying pan over medium heat. Add the oil, onion and
lemon rind and cook, stirring, for 6 minutes or until
soft. Add the kale and cook for 2 minutes or until wilted.
Add the spinach and cook for 1 minute or until soft. Add
the lemon juice, salt and pepper and stir to combine.

   Make 2 spaces in the greens mixture and break an
egg into each. Transfer the pan to the oven and bake
for 4–5 minutes or until the eggs are just set.

   Top the green eggs with the dill and chilli. Serve
with labne, a light sprinkling of sumac, lemon wedges
and flatbreads. SERVES 2

cook's note
I like to get creative with
my choice of greens for this
recipe (or sometimes to just
use up what's in my fridge!).
Try swapping out the kale
and adding rainbow chard
or silverbeet (Swiss chard)
instead. Trim and chop the
leaves of about 6 stalks,
depending on their size.

crispy chia salmon with za'atar salad

2 tablespoons extra virgin olive oil
2 teaspoons za'atar (see *cook's notes*)
sea salt and cracked black pepper
2 x 100g (3½ oz) skinless salmon fillets,
    2.5cm (1 in) thick
1 tablespoon black chia seeds
2 small cucumbers (250g/8¾ oz), halved
    and sliced lengthways
2 small beetroot (100g/3½ oz), peeled and thinly
    sliced using a mandolin
¼ cup (6g/¼ oz) dill sprigs
½ cup (140g/5 oz) plain Greek-style (thick) yoghurt
1 tablespoon lemon juice
lemon wedges, to serve

Preheat oven grill (broiler) to high. Line a small baking tray with aluminium foil.

Place the oil and za'atar in a small bowl, mix to combine and season with salt and pepper. Spoon half the za'atar mixture over the salmon to coat.

Place the chia seeds on a small flat plate. Press the underside of each salmon fillet into the chia seeds to coat and place, seed-side up, on the tray. Grill the salmon, without turning, for 4–5 minutes or until just cooked through. Allow to stand for 2 minutes.

While the salmon is cooking, divide the cucumber, beetroot, dill and yoghurt between serving plates. Add the lemon juice to the remaining za'atar mixture, stir to combine and drizzle over the salad. Top with the salmon and serve with lemon wedges. **SERVES 2**

cook's notes

I quite often switch up the fish that I use in this recipe, mostly depending on what's freshest at my fishmonger. The only rule is that it has to be a nice thick piece that won't dry out under the grill. Having said that, if you are using thinner pieces just reduce the grilling time!

Za'atar is a Middle-Eastern spice mix made from dried herbs, sesame seeds and sumac. Find it at spice shops and most supermarkets.

CHAPTER FIVE

basics

to

brilliance

If you know me, or you have my *basics to brilliance* books in YOUR KITCHEN, you'll know that this is *absolutely my thing* – it's what I'M ALL ABOUT! There is simply nothing *more powerful* than having an arsenal of basic, FEEL-GOOD recipes, that you can *call on anytime*, and using them as a SPRINGBOARD to create your *own repertoire* of NOURISHING MEALS. And as a *happy side-effect*? I think you'll find that it gives you a lot MORE CONFIDENCE in the kitchen.

broccoli dough

**600g (1 lb 5 oz) broccoli florets (about 2 heads),
  roughly chopped (see *cook's notes*)**
¾ cup (90g/3 oz) almond meal (ground almonds)
½ cup (25g/¾ oz) finely grated parmesan
3 eggs
sea salt and cracked black pepper

In small batches, place the broccoli in a food
processor and process until finely chopped.
Transfer to a large bowl.

  Add the almond meal, parmesan, eggs, salt
and pepper to the broccoli and mix well to
combine. **MAKES 1 QUANTITY**

cook's notes

It's best if you don't add too
much of the broccoli stem
to this dough. A floret with
roughly 6–8cm (3 in) of stem
is great. Adding extra can
make the dough watery.

You can swap half, or all, of
the broccoli for cauliflower
if you prefer. Again, just don't
use too much of the stem.

See the recipes that follow
for how to use this dough to
make a pizza, flatbread or tart.

broccoli margherita pizzas

1 x quantity broccoli dough (see *basic recipe*, page 146)
⅔ cup (50g/1¾ oz) finely grated parmesan
300g (10½ oz) cherry tomatoes, torn in half
  and squeezed to remove the seeds
¼ cup (4g/¼ oz) oregano leaves
extra virgin olive oil, for drizzling
2 x 125g (4½ oz) fresh mozzarella balls, torn
basil leaves, to serve
finely grated parmesan, extra, to serve (optional)

Preheat oven to 200°C (400°F). Line 2 x 30cm (12 in)
round oven trays with non-stick baking paper.

Divide the dough in half and press onto each tray
to make 2 x 28cm (11 in) round pizza bases. Bake for
20 minutes or until firm and slightly golden.

Sprinkle the bases with parmesan and top with
the tomatoes and oregano. Drizzle with a little oil.
Return the pizzas to the oven and bake for a further
20 minutes or until golden.

Top warm pizzas with the mozzarella and sprinkle
with basil and extra parmesan to serve. **SERVES 4**

cook's notes

You can add your favourite
toppings to this pizza, just
avoid anything that might
make the broccoli base turn
soft (like tomato puree) – it's
best to stick to fresh tomatoes
with the seeds and some of
the juice squeezed out. Try
sprinkling over pre-roasted
pumpkin, eggplant (aubergine)
or zucchini (courgette).

To have these pizza bases on
standby for busy days, bake
them for the first 20 minutes,
then cool, wrap and freeze
for later use.

broccoli flatbread salad sandwiches

1 x quantity broccoli dough (see *basic recipe*, page 146)
1 cup (260g/9 oz) store-bought or ready-prepared
  hummus, baba ghanoush or tzatziki
1 cup (120g/4¼ oz) grated carrot (about 1 carrot)
1 large cucumber, thinly sliced
80g (2¾ oz) snow pea sprouts
1 cup (100g/3½ oz) grated beetroot
  (about 1 small beetroot)
toasted pepitas (pumpkin seeds), sesame seeds
  and sunflower seeds, to serve (optional)
  (or see *honey seed sprinkle*, page 232)

Preheat oven to 180°C (350°F). Line 2 baking trays
with non-stick baking paper.

Divide the dough in half and press onto each tray
to make 2 even 20cm x 30cm (8 in x 12 in) rectangles.
Bake for 30–35 minutes or until golden. Allow to cool
on the trays for 10 minutes, before transferring onto
wire racks to cool completely.

Cut each flatbread rectangle into 4 pieces. Spread
4 of the pieces with hummus. Top with the carrot,
cucumber, sprouts and beetroot. Sprinkle with the
seed mix and top with the remaining flatbread pieces
to serve. **MAKES 4**

cook's note
Use these broccoli flatbreads
in the same way you would
any soft flatbread – make
wraps for lunchboxes, cut
them into small squares to
serve with dips, or team
them with an Indian curry.

broccoli, pumpkin, sage and goat's cheese tart

1 x quantity broccoli dough (see *basic recipe*, page 146)
800g (1 lb 12 oz) pumpkin, peeled and chopped
2 tablespoons extra virgin olive oil
sea salt and cracked black pepper
6 eggs
1 cup (240g/8½ oz) fresh ricotta
16–20 sage leaves
150g (5¼ oz) goat's cheese, broken into large pieces

Preheat oven to 200°C (400°F). Line 2 x 18cm-based 22cm-wide 3cm-high (7 in x 8½ in x 1 in) pie tins with non-stick baking paper. Line a large baking tray with non-stick baking paper.

Divide the dough in half and press evenly over the bases and sides of the pie tins. Place the pumpkin on the baking tray, drizzle with 1 tablespoon of the oil and sprinkle with salt and pepper. Bake the tart shells and pumpkin for 20 minutes or until golden.

Place the eggs, ricotta, salt and pepper in a large bowl and whisk to combine. Place the sage and the remaining 1 tablespoon of oil in a small bowl and toss to coat.

Divide the roasted pumpkin between the tart shells. Top with the egg mixture and sprinkle with the goat's cheese and sage. Bake for a further 25–30 minutes or until golden brown and the egg is set.

Allow tarts to cool slightly in the tins before lifting out and slicing into wedges to serve. **SERVES 6-8**

cook's notes

These tarts are great served either warm or at room temperature with a simple salad of greens.

The broccoli tart shell won't crumble like regular pastry, making it the perfect portable picnic food!

To add a smoky bacon flavour to the tarts, cook 4 trimmed and chopped rashers of bacon in a pan until golden. Sprinkle the bacon into the tart shells with the pumpkin.

spinach and zucchini fritters

4 cups (750g/1 lb 10 oz) firmly packed grated
   zucchini (courgette) (about 4 zucchinis)
1 cup (60g/2 oz) firmly packed finely chopped
   English spinach
½ cup (8g/¼ oz) mint leaves, shredded
5 eggs
¾ cup (90g/3 oz) almond meal (ground almonds)
½ cup (40g/1½ oz) finely grated parmesan
¼ cup (50g/1¾ oz) white chia seeds
sea salt and cracked black pepper
extra virgin olive oil, for cooking

Place the zucchini between sheets of absorbent kitchen
paper and press to remove any excess moisture.
   Place the zucchini, spinach, mint, eggs, almond meal,
parmesan, chia seeds, salt and pepper in a large bowl
and mix to combine. Allow to stand for 20–30 minutes.
   Heat an 18cm–20cm (7 in–8 in) non-stick frying pan
over medium-low heat. Add a little oil and ½ cup of the
fritter mixture. Spread the mixture thinly to cover the
base of the pan. Cook for 6–8 minutes each side or
until golden. Remove the fritter from the pan and place
on a sheet of non-stick baking paper. Repeat with the
remaining mixture, adding more oil as necessary, to
make 8 fritters. **MAKES 1 QUANTITY**

cook's notes

The secret to turning these
crispy fritters is to let them
cook for the full 6 minutes
on each side – don't be
tempted to flip too early!

You can wrap any leftover
fritters and keep them in
the fridge. When ready to
use, cover and warm them
slightly in the oven.

See the recipes that follow
for some super-fresh meal
ideas that use these crispy
fritters as a base.

avocado, black bean and tomato tacos

1 x 400g (14 oz) can black beans, drained and rinsed
400g (14 oz) cherry tomatoes, torn and squeezed
   to remove the seeds
1 red onion, finely chopped
2 teaspoons finely grated lime rind
¼ cup (60ml/2 fl oz) lime juice
½ cup (6g/¼ oz) coriander (cilantro) leaves
½ cup (12g/½ oz) small flat-leaf parsley leaves
sea salt and cracked black pepper
2 avocados, roughly chopped
1 x quantity spinach and zucchini fritters
   (see *basic recipe*, page 154)
1 long red chilli, seeded, sliced and fried, to serve

Place the beans, tomatoes and onion in a large bowl.
Add the lime rind and juice, coriander, parsley, salt and
pepper and mix gently to combine. Add the avocado
and fold to combine.
   Divide the mixture between the fritters and top
with the fried chilli to serve. **SERVES 4**

cook's notes
Get creative and pile the
tacos high with your own
combinations. Try adding
crispy pan-fried fish or
shredded cooked chicken
with some crunchy lettuce
and chilli mayo.

It's best to fill the tacos
just before serving to keep
them from turning too soft.

watercress, salmon and pickled onion crispy pancakes

1 x quantity spinach and zucchini fritters
   (see *basic recipe*, page 154)
4 cups (80g/2¾ oz) watercress sprigs
300g (10½ oz) smoked or cured salmon or trout
cracked black pepper, for sprinkling
dill tzatziki
2 small cucumbers (230g/8 oz), grated
⅓ cup (8g/¼ oz) dill sprigs, chopped
1½ cups (420g/15 oz) plain Greek-style (thick) yoghurt
1 teaspoon cracked black pepper
quick pickled red onions
2 red onions, finely sliced into rings
1 cup (250ml/8½ fl oz) white wine vinegar
sea salt and cracked black pepper

To make the quick pickled red onions, place the
onion, vinegar, salt and pepper in a non-reactive
(glass or ceramic) bowl and allow to stand for
20 minutes.

   While the onions are pickling, make the dill tzatziki.
Place the cucumber between layers of absorbent
kitchen paper and press to remove any excess
moisture. Transfer to a medium bowl. Add the dill,
yoghurt and pepper and mix to combine.

   Divide the fritters between serving plates and
spread with the tzatziki. Top with the watercress,
salmon and pickled onions and sprinkle with pepper.
Serve immediately. **SERVES 4**

cook's notes

You can swap the smoked
trout for thin slices of
prosciutto, bresaola or
rare-roasted beef.

I'll often make extra pickled
onions and store them in a
glass container in the fridge.
Use them in salads, on burgers
or as a zingy side to grilled
fish, meat or vegetables.

edamame avo smash super-green fritters

1 x quantity spinach and zucchini fritters
(see *basic recipe*, page 154)
1 x quantity edamame avo smash
(see *recipe*, page 230)
240g (8½ oz) broccolini (sprouting broccoli),
trimmed and blanched
½ cup (12g/½ oz) small red-veined sorrel leaves
¾ cup (210g/7½ oz) labne or plain Greek-style
(thick) yoghurt
extra virgin olive oil, for drizzling
sea salt and cracked black pepper

Divide the fritters between serving plates and
top with the edamame avo smash and broccolini.
Sprinkle with the sorrel leaves.

Place a large spoonful of the labne onto each
frittata, making a small indent with the back of
the spoon. Drizzle the labne with oil and sprinkle
with salt and pepper to serve. **SERVES 4**

cook's note
We so often associate green
vegies with lunch or dinner,
but I'm quite partial to serving
these feel-good fritters for
breakfast, too – especially
on a Saturday! Just add
soft-poached eggs in place
of the labne and top with a
little fresh chilli if you like it.

tomato and mozzarella tortillas with mint and basil oil

1 x quantity spinach and zucchini fritters
  (see *basic recipe*, page 154)
700g (1 lb 9 oz) mixed tomatoes, sliced
4 x 80g (2¾ oz) burrata or fresh mozzarella balls
sea salt and cracked black pepper
basil leaves, to serve
mint and basil oil
¼ cup (4g/¼ oz) mint leaves
¼ cup (5g/¼ oz) basil leaves
½ cup (125ml/4¼ fl oz) extra virgin olive oil
sea salt flakes

To make the mint and basil oil, place the mint, basil, oil and salt in a blender and blend until smooth.

   Divide the fritters between serving plates and top with the tomato, burrata, salt and pepper. Spoon the mint and basil oil over each tortilla and sprinkle with basil leaves to serve. **SERVES 4**

cook's notes
You can add paper-thin slices of bresaola or prosciutto to the top of these tortillas.

If I'm in a hurry, I'll replace the mint and basil oil with a good-quality store-bought basil pesto – easy!

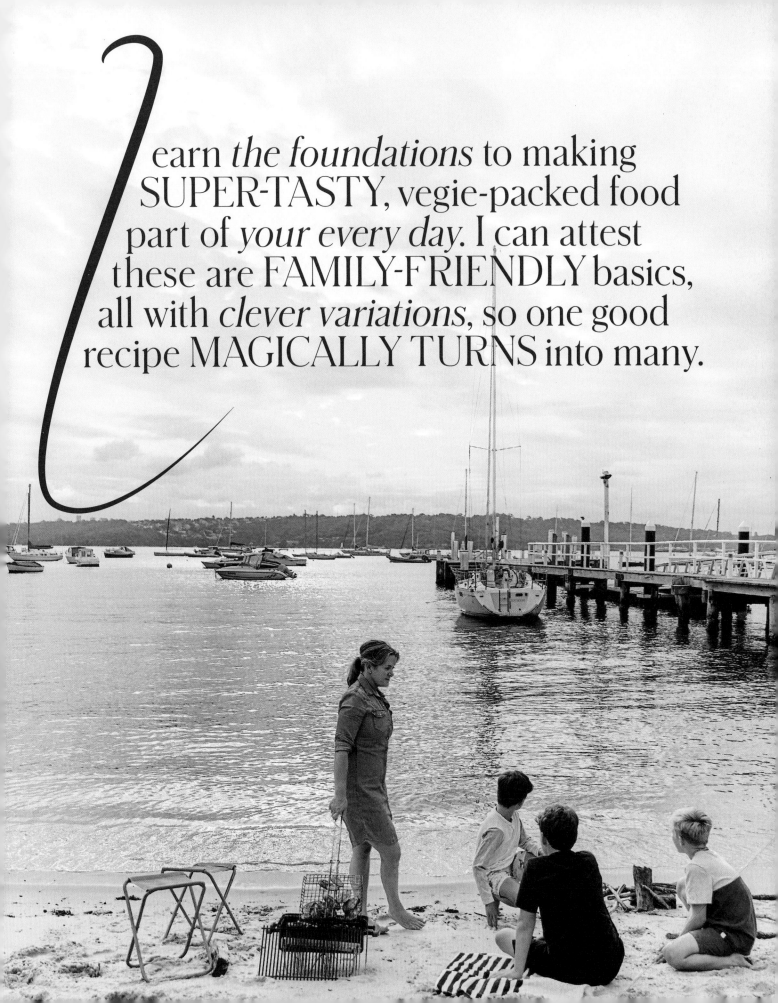

*L*earn *the foundations* to making SUPER-TASTY, vegie-packed food part of *your every day*. I can attest these are FAMILY-FRIENDLY basics, all with *clever variations*, so one good recipe MAGICALLY TURNS into many.

oat pastry

1 cup (90g/3 oz) rolled oats
¼ cup (50g/1¾ oz) white chia seeds
½ teaspoon fine table salt
1 cup (140g/5 oz) wholemeal (whole-wheat) spelt flour
½ cup (60g/2 oz) almond meal (ground almonds)
⅓ cup (80ml/2¾ fl oz) light-flavoured extra
   virgin olive oil
¼ cup (60ml/2 fl oz) water (or maple syrup
   for a sweet pastry) (see *cook's notes*)

Place the oats, chia seeds and salt in a food processor and process for 1 minute or until the mixture resembles fine breadcrumbs. Add the flour and almond meal and pulse to combine.

   Place the oil and water in a small jug and whisk to combine. With the food processor running, gradually add the oil mixture to the oat mixture and process until well combined but still crumbly. **MAKES 1 QUANTITY**

cook's notes
See the recipes that follow for how to use this pastry to make really versatile small and large tart shells, plus a super-simple galette base.

I've added the option of maple syrup in this recipe, specifically for the peachy plum tarts on page 172 – but you can use this trick whenever you're making something sweet with the oat pastry.

summer tomato and ricotta tart

1 x quantity oat pastry (see *basic recipe*, page 166)
1 cup (240g/8½ oz) fresh ricotta
2 teaspoons finely grated lemon rind
½ cup (40g/1½ oz) finely grated parmesan
sea salt and cracked black pepper
400g (14 oz) heirloom tomatoes, sliced
½ cup (10g/¼ oz) small basil leaves
extra virgin olive oil, for drizzling

Preheat oven to 180°C (350°F). Spoon the pastry into
a 24cm-based 3cm-high (9½ in x 1 in) round loose-based
fluted tart tin and press firmly over the base and sides
until smooth. Prick the pastry base all over with a fork
and bake for 20 minutes or until light golden.

While the tart shell is baking, place the ricotta, lemon
rind, parmesan, salt and pepper in a large bowl and mix
to combine.

Allow the tart shell to cool completely before carefully
lifting it from the tin. Place on a serving plate and fill
with the ricotta mixture. Top the tart with the tomato
and basil. Drizzle with oil, sprinkle with salt and pepper
and slice into wedges to serve. **SERVES 6**

cook's notes

I usually serve this simple
tart at room temperature
with a peppery rocket
(arugula) salad.

To ensure the pastry stays
extra crisp, add the ricotta
mixture and tomatoes
just before serving.

You can fill this tart shell
with your choice of sweet
or savoury fillings – from
cheeses, to roast vegetables,
to stone fruits. It works best
with firmer (as opposed to
liquid) ingredients.

fig, rocket and goat's cheese galette

1 x quantity oat pastry (see *basic recipe*, page 166)
150g (5¼ oz) goat's cheese or soft feta, crumbled
100g (3½ oz) wild rocket (arugula)
3 figs, torn in half
extra virgin olive oil, for drizzling
1 tablespoon vincotto (see *cook's notes*), for drizzling
sea salt and cracked black pepper

Preheat oven to 180°C (350°F). Line a large baking tray with non-stick baking paper.

Turn the pastry out and bring it together to form a ball. Place on the tray and press out to form a rough 20cm x 30cm (8 in x 12 in) rectangle. Prick the base all over with a fork. Bake for 20 minutes or until golden. Allow to cool completely on the tray.

Top the galette base evenly with the goat's cheese, rocket and figs. Drizzle with oil and the vincotto. Sprinkle with salt and pepper to serve. **SERVES 4**

cook's notes

If you can't find vincotto you can use caramelised balsamic vinegar or balsamic glaze, for its tangy but sweet flavour.

Try swapping in very thinly sliced pear (or apple) if figs are out of season.

peachy plum tarts

1 x quantity oat pastry (see *basic recipe*, page 166),
   made with maple syrup
1 cup (280g/10 oz) plain Greek-style (thick) yoghurt
2 tablespoons honey, plus extra for drizzling
2 ripe peaches, thinly sliced
2 ripe plums, thinly sliced
1 vanilla bean, split and seeds scraped

Preheat oven to 180°C (350°F). Divide the pastry
between 6 x 6.5cm-based 10cm-wide 1.5cm-high
(2½ in x 4 in x ½ in) fluted shallow pie tins (see *cook's
notes*) and press the mixture evenly over the bases
and sides. Prick the pastry all over with a fork.
Place the tart shells on a baking tray and bake for
20 minutes or until golden. Allow to cool completely
in the tins before turning out onto a serving plate.
   Place the yoghurt and honey in a small bowl, mix
to combine and spoon into the tart shells. Divide
the peach and plum slices between the tarts and
drizzle with extra honey. Top the tarts with the
vanilla seeds to serve. **MAKES 6**

cook's notes
If you don't have pie tins to
match the size I've used here,
you can bake 4 (instead of 6)
slightly larger tarts instead
– use 10cm-based 12cm-wide
3cm-high (4 in x 4½ in x 1 in)
pie tins.

I make these pretty, summery
tarts all year round, but I'll
use whatever fruit is in season
– think berries, figs or finely
sliced pear.

choc-chunk tahini cookies

1 cup (280g/10 oz) hulled tahini (see *cook's notes*)
1 cup (220g/7¾ oz) raw caster (superfine) sugar
⅓ cup (80ml/2¾ fl oz) maple syrup
2 teaspoons vanilla extract
1 egg
2 cups (280g/10 oz) wholemeal (whole-wheat)
  spelt flour
¼ teaspoon bicarbonate of (baking) soda
¼ teaspoon baking powder
200g (7 oz) chopped dark chocolate

Preheat oven to 160°C (325°F). Line 2 large baking
trays with non-stick baking paper.

Place the tahini, sugar, maple syrup, vanilla and egg
in a large bowl and mix well to combine.

Place the flour, bicarbonate of soda and baking
powder in a medium bowl and stir to combine. Sift
the flour mixture into the tahini mixture and mix well
to combine. Add the chocolate and fold to combine.

Roll heaped tablespoons of the dough into 24 balls
and place on the trays. Flatten the cookies slightly
and bake for 12–14 minutes or until light golden.
Allow to cool on the trays. **MAKES 1 QUANTITY**

cook's notes
This recipe works best when
a smooth, thick, hulled tahini
is used. Avoid those jars that
have fully settled on the shelf
(with a large layer of oil at
the top and dried-out tahini
underneath). Look for a fresh,
good-quality, blended variety.

You can swap the spelt flour
for buckwheat flour to make
these cookies gluten free. Just
double check your baking
powder is gluten free too!

double choc-chunk share cookies

⅓ cup (35g/1¼ oz) raw cacao or cocoa powder
1 x quantity choc-chunk tahini cookie dough
  (see *basic recipe*, page 174)
60g (2 oz) white chocolate, roughly chopped

Preheat oven to 160°C (325°F). Lightly grease
2 x 22cm (8½ in) heavy-based ovenproof frying pans
(skillets) (see *cook's notes*).
  Sift the cacao into the cookie dough mixture
(with the dry ingredients) and mix well to combine.
Add the white chocolate (with the dark chocolate)
and fold to combine.
  Divide the cookie dough in half and press evenly
into the skillets. Bake for 15 minutes or until firm
to the touch. **MAKES 2**

cook's notes

If you only have 1 skillet,
simply bake the cookies in
2 batches. If you don't have a
skillet, you can line 2 baking
trays with non-stick baking
paper. Shape each half of the
dough into a 22cm (8½ in)
round and place on the trays.

To make regular-sized cookies,
line 2 large baking trays with
non-stick baking paper. Roll
heaped tablespoons of the
dough into 24 balls and place
on the trays. Flatten slightly
and bake for 12–14 minutes
or until light golden. Allow
to cool on the trays.

coconut and sour cherry chocolate drizzle cookies

¾ cup (110g/4 oz) dried sour cherries (see *cook's note*)
1 cup (75g/2½ oz) shredded coconut
1 x quantity choc-chunk tahini cookie dough (see
  ***basic recipe*, page 174), chocolate not-yet added**

Preheat oven to 160°C (325°F). Line 2 large baking trays with non-stick baking paper.

Add the cherries and coconut to the cookie dough (reserving the chocolate for melting later) and fold to combine. Roll heaped tablespoons of the dough into 26 balls and place on the trays. Flatten the cookies slightly and bake for 12–14 minutes or until golden. Allow to cool on the trays.

While the cookies are cooling, place the chocolate in a small saucepan over medium heat and stir until melted and smooth.

Use a spoon to drizzle the chocolate over the cooled cookies and allow to set before serving. **MAKES 26**

cook's note
Dried sour cherries have a sweet but tart flavour – I love the extra chewiness they add to these cookies. They're sold in most supermarkets, but if you can't find them, swap in dried cranberries instead.

choc-chunk cookie ice-cream sandwiches

6 bananas, thinly sliced
¼ cup (70g/2½ oz) coconut yoghurt or plain
  Greek-style (thick) yoghurt
1 tablespoon vanilla extract
1 x quantity choc-chunk tahini cookies
  (see *basic recipe*, page 174)

Place the banana slices in the freezer for 6 hours or overnight, until solid.

Place the banana, yoghurt and vanilla in a food processor and process until smooth. Scoop into a metal container and freeze for 30 minutes or until just firm.

Place scoops of ice-cream onto the underside of half the cookies. Sandwich with the remaining cookies. Freeze for a further 30 minutes or until firm, before serving. **MAKES 12**

cook's note
When you have an abundance of ripe bananas in your fruit bowl, why not peel, slice and put some in the freezer. That way, you'll be ready to make this cheat's ice-cream whenever you feel like it!

Once you *master the basics,* I think you'll FEEL MORE *spontaneous and creative* with your choice of *fresh ingredients.* And that means using more of what's IN SEASON, in your fridge or *in your garden* – great!

crunchy granola

1½ cups (135g/4¾ oz) rolled oats (see *cook's notes*)
⅔ cup (80g/2¾ oz) pecans or walnuts, finely chopped
1 cup (120g/4¼ oz) almond meal (ground almonds)
½ cup (80g/2¾ oz) pepitas (pumpkin seeds)
½ cup (80g/2¾ oz) sunflower seeds
½ cup (40g/1½ oz) shredded coconut
1 teaspoon ground cinnamon
⅓ cup (80ml/2¾ fl oz) maple syrup
¼ cup (60ml/2 fl oz) extra virgin olive oil
2 teaspoons vanilla extract

Preheat oven to 180°C (350°F). Place the oats, pecans, almond meal, pepitas, sunflower seeds, coconut and cinnamon in a large bowl and mix to combine. Add the maple syrup, oil and vanilla and mix gently to coat.

Divide the mixture between 2 baking trays and spread evenly. Bake for 15 minutes. Stir the mixture and bake for a further 10–15 minutes or until the granola is golden and crunchy. Allow to cool on the trays. **MAKES 1 QUANTITY**

cook's notes

If you'd like to make a gluten-free granola, swap the regular rolled oats for gluten-free oats. These are available at specialty food stores and health food shops – just be sure to check the labels.

This recipe makes about 9 cups of granola. Store it in an airtight container to snack on or serve it for breakfast with fruit and yoghurt. See the recipes that follow for how to use it to bake treats.

mixed berry granola crumbles

2 cups (250g/8¾ oz) fresh or frozen raspberries
2 cups (250g/8¾ oz) fresh or frozen blueberries
2 cups (250g/8¾ oz) fresh or frozen strawberries
2 apples, cored and finely chopped
2 tablespoons cornflour (cornstarch)
¼ cup (55g/2 oz) raw caster (superfine) sugar
2 teaspoons vanilla extract
1 x quantity crunchy granola mixture
  (see *basic recipe*, page 184), uncooked

Preheat oven to 160°C (325°F). Place the raspberries, blueberries, strawberries and apple in a large bowl and toss to combine. Sift the cornflour over the fruit and gently mix to combine. Add the sugar and vanilla and fold to combine.

  Divide the fruit mixture between 8 x 1-cup-capacity (250ml/8½ fl oz) ovenproof dishes. Place the dishes onto baking trays. Divide the uncooked granola evenly between the dishes, piling it high on top of the fruit. Bake for 25–30 minutes or until golden and crunchy and the fruit is bubbling. MAKES 8

cook's notes
Serve these toasty berry crumbles warm or cold with spoonfuls of vanilla or plain Greek-style (thick) yoghurt.

You can swap the berries for whichever fruits you like – try chopped mango, pear or banana.

blueberry granola cookies

½ cup (125g/4½ oz) cashew or almond butter
⅓ cup (80ml/2¾ fl oz) maple syrup (see *cook's notes*)
¾ cup (150g/5¼ oz) dried blueberries
   (see *cook's notes*)
1 x quantity crunchy granola mixture
   (see *basic recipe*, page 184), uncooked

Preheat oven to 180°C (350°F). Line 2 large baking trays with non-stick baking paper.
   Add the cashew butter, maple syrup and blueberries to the uncooked granola and mix to combine. Shape ¼-cup portions of the mixture into balls. Place on the trays and flatten slightly. Bake for 20 minutes or until golden. Allow to cool on the trays. **MAKES 15**

cook's notes

Filled with nuts and seeds, these cookies are a great breakfast-on-the-go, plus they make the perfect post-workout snack.

The maple syrup that's called for in this recipe is in addition to the maple that's already in the basic granola mixture.

Feel free to swap the dried blueberries for some dried cranberries, strawberries or your favourite chopped dried fruit.

Store cookies in an airtight container for up to 2 weeks.

raspberry and apple granola slice

⅓ cup (80ml/2¾ fl oz) maple syrup (see *cook's notes*)
1 x quantity crunchy granola mixture
  (see *basic recipe*, page 184), uncooked
2 red or pink apples, cored and finely chopped
2 cups (250g/8¾ oz) fresh or frozen raspberries
2 teaspoons cornflour (cornstarch)
¼ cup (55g/2 oz) raw caster (superfine) sugar
1 teaspoon vanilla extract

Preheat oven to 180°C (350°F). Line a 20cm x 30cm
(8 in x 12 in) slice tin with non-stick baking paper.
  Add the maple syrup to the uncooked granola and
mix to combine. Press three-quarters of the granola
mixture firmly into the base of the tin.
  Place the apple and raspberries in a large bowl and
toss to combine. Sift the cornflour over the fruit and
gently mix to combine. Add the sugar and vanilla and
fold to combine. Spoon the fruit mixture evenly into
the tin. Sprinkle with the remaining granola mixture.
  Bake for 35–40 minutes or until the top is golden
and crunchy. Allow to cool in the tin before slicing to
serve. **SERVES 10–12**

cook's notes
This recipe makes a soft
dessert slice. It's very easily
made with any combination
of fruits – try pear and
blueberry, or apple, pear
and mixed berry.

The maple syrup that's called
for in this recipe is in addition
to the maple that's already in
the basic granola mixture.

I like to serve this fruity slice
warm or cold, with spoonfuls
of vanilla-bean or plain
Greek-style (thick) yoghurt.

CHAPTER SIX

there's
always
room
for

sweets

or as long as I can remember, my *mantra in life* has been AROUND BALANCE. I think we should enjoy *everything in moderation,* and that definitely includes SWEET TREATS. Yes, sugar has been given *a bad rap* recently, but I won't compromise on FLAVOUR. So, these *cookies, cakes, tarts, slices* and more all still deliver BIG PUNCHY TASTE, but with a *bit less sugar.* They're the recipes WE ALL LOVE, made with more *fresh produce* and a few CLEVER INGREDIENT swaps along the way.

lemon thyme, honey and almond cake

¾ cup (270g/9½ oz) honey
4 eggs
¼ cup (60ml/2 fl oz) light-flavoured extra
   virgin olive oil
1 tablespoon lemon thyme leaves
1 tablespoon finely grated lemon rind
¼ cup (60ml/2 fl oz) lemon juice
3 cups (360g/12½ oz) almond meal (ground almonds)
1 teaspoon baking powder
extra honey, for drizzling
extra lemon thyme sprigs, to serve
plain Greek-style (thick) yoghurt, to serve (optional)

Preheat oven to 160°C (325°F). Line a 22cm (8½ in) round springform tin with non-stick baking paper.

Place the honey and eggs in a large bowl and whisk to combine. Add the oil, lemon thyme, lemon rind and juice and whisk to combine. Add the almond meal and baking powder and whisk until smooth.

Pour the mixture into the tin and bake for 35–40 minutes or until golden and cooked when tested with a skewer. Allow to cool in the tin for 10 minutes.

Remove the cake from the tin and place on a cake stand or plate. Drizzle with extra honey and scatter with extra thyme sprigs. Cut into wedges and serve with yoghurt. SERVES 12

cook's note
This lemony cake is one of my most requested recipes. It's also the cake I make when I need to prep something sweet in advance – it's dense and moist, meaning it keeps well, plus I find the flavours continue to develop over time. Store it in an airtight container for up to 10 days.

choc-fudge popsicles

1¾ cups (430ml/14½ fl oz) coconut cream,
  at room temperature
75g (2½ oz) dark (70% cocoa) chocolate, melted
2 teaspoons vanilla extract
6 soft fresh dates (120g/4¼ oz), pitted

Place the coconut cream, chocolate, vanilla and
dates in a blender and blend until smooth.
  Divide the mixture between 8 x ⅓-cup-capacity
(80ml/2¾ fl oz) popsicle moulds. Insert popsicle
sticks and freeze for 2 hours or until solid. **MAKES 8**

cook's note
The best way to remove the
frozen popsicles is to place
the moulds under warm
(not hot) running water for a
few seconds. Allow them to
stand for another 30 seconds
and they should release easily.

lemon and yoghurt baked cheesecake

1 cup (120g/4¼ oz) almond meal (ground almonds)
2 tablespoons coconut sugar
¼ cup (40g/1½ oz) brown rice flour
80g (2¾ oz) unsalted butter, melted
yoghurt and ricotta filling
1¾ cups (420g/15 oz) fresh ricotta
250g (8¾ oz) cream cheese
¾ cup (165g/6 oz) raw caster (superfine) sugar
4 eggs
1½ tablespoons finely grated lemon rind
2½ teaspoons vanilla extract
2 tablespoons cornflour (cornstarch)
2 tablespoons lemon juice
1 cup (280g/10 oz) plain Greek-style (thick) yoghurt
coconut lemon curd
1 cup (250ml/8½ fl oz) coconut cream
2 tablespoons lemon juice
⅓ cup (75g/2½ oz) raw caster (superfine) sugar

Preheat oven to 180°C (350°F). Line a 22cm (8½ in) round springform tin with non-stick baking paper.

Place the almond meal, coconut sugar, flour and butter in a large bowl and mix to combine. Press the mixture evenly into the base of the tin and bake for 15 minutes or until golden.

To make the yoghurt and ricotta filling, place the ricotta, cream cheese and sugar in a food processor and process until smooth and the sugar has dissolved. Add the eggs, lemon rind and vanilla and process until just combined. Place the cornflour and lemon juice in a small bowl and mix until smooth. Add the cornflour mixture to the filling and process until combined. Add the yoghurt and very gently fold to combine.

Reduce the oven temperature to 140°C (275°F). Pour the filling onto the base in the tin. Bake for 45 minutes or until the filling is almost set but with a wobble in the centre (see *cook's note*). Allow to cool in the tin at room temperature for 30 minutes, before refrigerating for 3 hours or until set.

While the cheesecake is baking, make the coconut lemon curd. Place the coconut cream, lemon juice and sugar in a medium saucepan over low heat. Cook, stirring constantly, for 20–22 minutes or until reduced and thickened. Allow to cool slightly and refrigerate until cold.

Remove the cheesecake from the tin and place on a cake stand or plate. Top with the coconut lemon curd and cut into wedges to serve. SERVES 10–12

cook's note
I have a few tricks to achieving a perfect, velvety smooth cheesecake (without a crack!). The first one is to only bake the cake for the recommended time – it will have a serious wobble in the centre, but that will set as it cools. Secondly, if you allow the cheesecake to cool at room temperature for 30 minutes before placing it in the fridge, it reduces that rapid change in temperature, meaning less chance of cracks.

peach and coconut tarts

4 x 20cm (8 in) wholemeal (whole-wheat) flour tortillas
⅓ cup (80ml/2¾ fl oz) maple syrup
¾ cup (60g/2 oz) shredded coconut
¼ cup (55g/2 oz) raw caster (superfine) sugar
2 teaspoons vanilla extract
2 large peaches, sliced into 1cm (½ in) wedges
1 cup (130g/4½ oz) fresh or frozen raspberries
plain Greek-style (thick) or vanilla bean yoghurt,
   to serve
extra maple syrup, to serve

Preheat oven to 180°C (350°F). Line 2 large baking
trays with non-stick baking paper.

Brush both sides of each tortilla with maple syrup
and place on the trays, reserving any remaining
syrup. Bake the tortillas for 5 minutes or until just
beginning to crisp.

Place the coconut, sugar and vanilla in a medium
bowl and mix to combine. Sprinkle the tortillas
evenly with the coconut mixture, leaving a 1cm (½ in)
border. Top with the peach wedges and scatter
with the raspberries. Drizzle with the remaining
maple syrup. Bake for 10 minutes or until the edges
are golden brown and the fruit has softened slightly.

Serve the tarts with yoghurt and extra maple
syrup. **MAKES 4**

cook's note
These cheat's tarts can be
topped with any kind of fruit
– the possibilities are endless!
I use all types of stone fruits
and whichever berries I have
on-hand.

chocolate and miso caramel slice

¼ cup (25g/1 oz) raw cacao or cocoa powder
⅓ cup (80g/2¾ oz) coconut oil, melted
¼ cup (60ml/2 fl oz) maple syrup
almond base
¾ cup (120g/4¼ oz) almonds
⅓ cup (25g/1 oz) desiccated coconut
6 soft fresh dates (120g/4¼ oz), pitted
¼ cup (60g/2 oz) smooth cashew butter
miso caramel
1½ cups (225g/8 oz) coconut sugar
1½ cups (375ml/12½ fl oz) coconut cream
½ cup (125g/4½ oz) smooth cashew butter
1 tablespoon white miso paste (shiro) (see *cook's notes*)
1 teaspoon vanilla extract

To make the almond base, line a 20cm (8 in) square cake tin with non-stick baking paper, allowing 4cm (1½ in) of the paper to overhang the sides. Place the almonds, coconut, dates and cashew butter in a food processor. Process for 1–2 minutes or until the mixture resembles fine breadcrumbs. Using the back of a spoon, press the mixture into the base of the tin and refrigerate for 30 minutes or until set.

Preheat oven to 160°C (325°F). To make the miso caramel, place the sugar, coconut cream, cashew butter, miso paste and vanilla in a large non-stick frying pan over medium heat. Cook, stirring constantly with a heatproof spatula, for 10 minutes or until thickened.

Pour the caramel evenly over the almond base and bake for 25 minutes. Allow to cool at room temperature for 10 minutes, before refrigerating until cold.

Place the cacao, oil and maple syrup in a medium heatproof bowl over a saucepan of simmering water (the bowl shouldn't touch the water) and stir for 2–3 minutes or until smooth. Pour the cacao mixture over the caramel and refrigerate for 30 minutes or until set.

Use the paper to help you lift the slice from the tin and cut into bars. Refrigerate until ready to serve. **MAKES 30**

cook's notes

This slice is best eaten almost straight from the fridge. If I'm serving it to a crowd, I'll usually cut it into squares, place them on a platter and then into the refrigerator, so the pieces firm up nicely in advance.

For a saltier caramel, simply add a little extra miso paste.

You can use smooth almond butter in place of the cashew butter, if you prefer.

Keep the slice in an airtight container in the fridge for up to 2 weeks.

cinnamon almond cookies

1¼ cups (150g/5¼ oz) almond meal (ground almonds)
1 cup (250g/8¾ oz) almond butter
¾ cup (110g/4 oz) coconut sugar
¼ cup (60ml/2 fl oz) maple syrup
2 teaspoons vanilla extract
1 teaspoon ground cinnamon
12 blanched almonds
chai tea, to serve (optional)

Preheat oven to 160°C (325°F). Line a large baking tray with non-stick baking paper.

Place the almond meal, almond butter, sugar, maple syrup, vanilla and cinnamon in a large bowl and mix to combine.

Roll 1-tablespoon portions of the mixture into balls, flatten slightly and place on the tray. Press an almond into the top of each cookie. Bake for 12–14 minutes or until deep golden in colour (see *cook's notes*). Allow to cool on the trays. Serve with chai tea. **MAKES 12**

cook's note
Don't be afraid to bake these cookies until they're deep golden in colour – you'll be rewarded with the most incredible caramelised flavour. That little extra time in the oven also keeps the cookies crisp on the outside and fudgy on the inside for more than a day – if they last that long!

chocolate and raspberry cupcakes

2 teaspoons vanilla extract
½ cup (125ml/4¼ fl oz) maple syrup
¼ cup (60ml/2 fl oz) milk
⅓ cup (80ml/2¾ fl oz) light-flavoured extra virgin
  olive oil
2 eggs
2 cups (240g/8½ oz) almond meal (ground almonds)
1 teaspoon baking powder
⅓ cup (35g/1¼ oz) raw cacao or cocoa powder
¾ cup (100g/3½ oz) fresh or frozen raspberries

Preheat oven to 160°C (325°F). Line 8 x ½-cup-capacity
(125ml/4¼ fl oz) muffin tins with paper cases.
  Place the vanilla, maple syrup, milk, oil and eggs in a
medium jug and whisk to combine.
  Place the almond meal, baking powder and cacao in
a large bowl and mix to combine. Add the maple mixture
to the dry ingredients and mix to combine.
  Fill each tin half-full with the cupcake mixture. Sprinkle
with the raspberries and top with the remaining mixture.
Bake for 20–22 minutes or until firm to the touch.
Allow to cool completely in the tins. before lifting out
the cupcakes to serve. MAKES 8

cook's notes

What's not to love about
chocolate and raspberries
together – it's a match made
in heaven! These cupcakes
work just as well with fresh as
they do frozen berries, so use
whichever you have on-hand.

This recipe is gluten free – if
you have intolerances, just be
sure to check that your baking
powder is gluten free, too.

raspberry soft serve

2¼ cups (290g/10¼ oz) frozen raspberries
2 tablespoons maple syrup
1 fresh eggwhite

Place the raspberries and maple syrup in a food
processor and process until smooth. Add the eggwhite
and process until the mixture is light and fluffy.

Spoon into serving bowls (see *cook's note*) and serve
immediately or place in an airtight container and freeze
for up to 2 days. **SERVES 4-6**

vanilla soft serve

2 cups (560g/1 lb 4 oz) plain Greek-style
   (thick) yoghurt
⅓ cup (80ml/2¾ fl oz) maple syrup
2 tablespoons vanilla extract
1 teaspoon vanilla bean paste

Place the yoghurt, maple syrup, vanilla extract and
vanilla bean paste in a large jug and whisk to combine.
Pour the mixture into ice-cube trays and freeze for
2–3 hours or until solid.

Release the frozen cubes into a food processor and
process until smooth. Transfer to a container and
return to the freezer for 1 hour or until slightly firm.

Spoon into serving bowls (see *cook's note*) and serve
immediately or freeze for up to 2 days. **SERVES 4-6**

cook's note
To present this treat like good
old-fashioned soft serve,
spoon the frozen mixture into
a piping bag that's fitted with a
star-shaped nozzle. Freeze for
a further 10 minutes then pipe
into bowls to serve.

passionfruit and coconut crème brûlée

¾ cup (180ml/6 fl oz) passionfruit pulp
  (about 6–8 passionfruit) (see *cook's notes*)
2 tablespoons maple syrup
2 tablespoons white chia seeds
2 tablespoons raw caster (superfine) sugar
coconut crème
1⅔ cups (400ml/13½ fl oz) coconut cream
¼ cup (50g/1¾ oz) white chia seeds
2 teaspoons vanilla bean paste
2 tablespoons maple syrup

Place the passionfruit, maple syrup and chia seeds in a medium bowl and mix to combine. Divide the mixture between 4 x 1-cup-capacity (250ml/8½ fl oz) heatproof dishes or ramekins. Allow to stand for 20 minutes or until thickened.

To make the coconut crème, place the coconut cream, chia seeds, vanilla and maple syrup in a blender and blend until smooth.

Carefully pour the coconut crème over the passionfruit mixture in the dishes and refrigerate for 3–4 hours or until set.

Sprinkle the surfaces with the sugar and, using a small kitchen blowtorch (see *cook's notes*), caramelise the tops to serve. **MAKES 4**

cook's notes

You can swap the passionfruit in this recipe for the same amount of crushed fresh raspberries – so tasty!

A little kitchen blowtorch is such a handy tool to have in your drawer. They're easy to master and mean you can add gorgeous golden crunch to desserts – super impressive. Find them at kitchenware stores and online.

raw caramel oat cookies

⅓ cup (55g/2 oz) sunflower seeds
⅓ cup (55g/2 oz) pepitas (pumpkin seeds)
2 tablespoons hemp seeds (optional)
1 cup (90g/3 oz) rolled oats
12 soft fresh dates (240g/8½ oz), pitted
½ cup (125g/4½ oz) cashew, almond or peanut butter
2 teaspoons vanilla extract
1½ teaspoons ground cinnamon
finely crushed pistachios, freeze-dried raspberries
  or cacao nibs, for sprinkling (see *cook's notes*)

Line a large tray with non-stick baking paper. Place
the sunflower seeds, pepitas, hemp seeds, oats,
dates, cashew butter, vanilla and cinnamon in a food
processor and process until a rough dough forms.
   Roll 1-tablespoon portions of the mixture into balls
and flatten slightly. Place on the tray, sprinkle with
pistachios, freeze-dried raspberries or cacao nibs
and refrigerate for 1 hour or until firm. **MAKES 20**

cook's notes
These cookies are what
I reach for when I need a
post-workout pick-me-up
or healthy snack on the go.

Keep them in the fridge in
an airtight container for up
to 1 week.

Choose your favourite
topping to sprinkle on the
cookies (or try all three!).
You'll need about ½ cup
in total.

pomegranate, strawberry and rosewater coconut wafers

¼ cup (90g/3 oz) honey
1½ teaspoons rosewater
1 cup (250g/8¾ oz) thick vanilla-bean
   or coconut yoghurt
250g (8¾ oz) strawberries, hulled and sliced
½ cup (80g/2¾ oz) pomegranate seeds
coconut wafers
1 cup (75g/2½ oz) shredded coconut
1 eggwhite
¼ cup (55g/2 oz) raw caster (superfine) sugar

To make the coconut wafers, preheat oven to
160°C (325°F). Line 2 baking trays with non-stick
baking paper. Place the coconut, eggwhite and sugar
in a medium bowl and mix to combine. Spoon the
mixture onto the trays to make 8 x 8cm (3 in) rounds,
flattening them slightly using the back of the spoon.
Bake for 12–14 minutes or until light golden. Allow
to cool on the trays.

   Place the honey and rosewater in a small bowl and
mix to combine. Place 4 of the coconut wafers onto
serving plates. Top with the yoghurt, strawberries
and pomegranate and drizzle with the honey mixture.
Top with the remaining wafers to serve. **MAKES 4**

cook's note
You can make the coconut
wafers up to 4 days in advance
and store them, unfilled, in an
airtight container. It's a great
option if you're entertaining
– simply assemble and serve.

pineapple coconut sherbet

2½ cups (375g/13¼ oz) chopped pineapple
   (about half a pineapple)
¾ cup (180ml/6 fl oz) coconut water
¼ cup (60g/2 oz) coconut yoghurt
2 tablespoons lime juice
2 tablespoons maple syrup
½ cup (125g/4½ oz) coconut yoghurt, extra
½ cup (25g/1 oz) toasted coconut flakes

Place the pineapple, coconut water, yoghurt, lime juice and maple syrup in a blender and blend until smooth. Strain the mixture through a fine sieve into a shallow non-reactive (glass, ceramic or plastic) dish, discarding any solids, and freeze for 4 hours or until frozen.

Using a fork, scrape the surface of the sherbet to create ice-crystals. Return to the freezer until ready to serve.

Divide the sherbet between serving bowls and top with the extra coconut yoghurt and coconut flakes to serve. **SERVES 6**

cook's note
Cool zingy pineapple ice crystals, topped with creamy coconut, make this sweet treat taste like pure summer. It's my go-to dessert for barbecues and post-beach entertaining.

raw carrot cake cashew bites

1 cup (150g/5¼ oz) raw cashews
1 cup (120g/4¼ oz) grated carrot (about 1 carrot)
10 soft fresh dates (200g/7 oz), pitted
⅓ cup (25g/1 oz) desiccated coconut
½ teaspoon finely grated ginger
1 teaspoon ground cinnamon
½ teaspoon mixed spice
½ cup (60g/2 oz) finely chopped walnuts or pecans

Place the cashews, carrot, dates, coconut, ginger, cinnamon and mixed spice in a food processor and process until combined.

Place the chopped walnuts on a small tray. Shape 1-tablespoon portions of the carrot mixture into balls and roll in the nuts to coat. Refrigerate until ready to serve. **MAKES 16**

cook's notes
These tiny treats are my latest weakness – think all the flavour of a carrot cake packed into one raw little bite. So easy to make, so addictive!

Keep your stash of these tasty bites in an airtight container in the fridge for up to 1 week.

CHAPTER SEVEN

the
foundations

*J*ust because they're *spooned over*, served at the side or SPRINKLED ON TOP of my recipes at the very *last second*, doesn't mean they're not important! In fact, I've named these tangy pickles, CREAMY SAUCES, zingy dressings and *cooling drinks* THE FOUNDATIONS because, in my mind, *they're essential.* Want to know the BEST PART? These finishing touches have been made with *savvy superfood* swaps, so it's ALL GOOD.

pickled vegetables

¾ cup (180ml/6 fl oz) water
¾ cup (180ml/6 fl oz) rice wine vinegar
¾ cup (180ml/6 fl oz) apple cider or white
  wine vinegar
1 tablespoon raw caster (superfine) sugar
1½ teaspoons sea salt flakes
flavour options
1 teaspoon fennel seeds
1 teaspoon juniper berries, lightly crushed
2 sprigs dill
2 sprigs tarragon
vegetable options
500g (1 lb 2 oz) beetroot, peeled and finely sliced
750g (1 lb 10 oz) radishes, trimmed and finely sliced
700g (1 lb 9 oz) baby carrots, trimmed, peeled
  and halved lengthways
500g (1 lb 2 oz) red onion, thinly sliced
300g (10½ oz) rainbow chard, stalks trimmed
500g (1 lb 2 oz) baby cucumbers, quartered

Place the water, rice wine vinegar, apple cider vinegar, sugar and salt in a medium saucepan over medium-high heat and bring to the boil. Add your choice of flavour options (see *cook's notes*) and simmer for 1 minute. Allow to cool for 5 minutes.

Place the vegetable of your choice (see *cook's notes*) into a 3-cup-capacity (750ml/25 fl oz) clean, dry heatproof jar or divide between 2 x 1½-cup-capacity (375ml/12½ fl oz) clean, dry heatproof jars.

Top with the hot pickling liquid, leaving a 1cm (½ in) space at the top of each jar. Seal with tight-fitting lids and refrigerate for up to 3 weeks. **MAKES 3 CUPS**

cook's notes

Use as many flavours as you like for the pickled vegetables (or you can leave them plain). There's enough pickling liquid in this recipe for you to choose 1 quantity of vegetables. I like to pair carrots with fennel seeds, cucumber with the juniper berries, beetroot with tarragon and the rainbow chard with dill – but use what you have to create what you like!

Eat the pickled veg as early as 2 hours after you've jarred them, or let the flavours develop in the fridge and use within 3 weeks.

tahini dressing

½ cup (140g/5 oz) hulled tahini
¼ cup (60ml/2 fl oz) lemon juice
2 tablespoons apple cider vinegar
1 tablespoon white miso paste (shiro)
¼ cup (60ml/2 fl oz) water
1 clove garlic, crushed
1½ teaspoons honey

Place the tahini, lemon juice, vinegar, miso paste, water, garlic and honey in a blender and blend until smooth and creamy. **MAKES 1 CUP**

green dressing

1 cup (24g/¾ oz) flat-leaf parsley leaves
1 cup (16g/½ oz) mint leaves
¼ cup (60ml/2 fl oz) lemon juice
2 green onions (scallions), trimmed and chopped
¾ cup (210g/7½ oz) plain Greek-style (thick) yoghurt
½ small clove garlic
sea salt and cracked black pepper

Place the parsley, mint, lemon juice, onion, yoghurt and garlic in a food processor or blender and process until smooth. Season with salt and pepper. **MAKES 1⅔ CUPS**

creamy cashew sauce

1 cup (150g/5¼ oz) raw cashews
2 cups (500ml/17 fl oz) boiling water
½ cup (125ml/4¼ fl oz) cold water
⅓ cup (80ml/2¾ fl oz) lemon juice
1 teaspoon honey
2 tablespoons soy sauce or coconut aminos
1 clove garlic, roughly chopped

Place the cashews in a medium heatproof bowl and cover with the boiling water. Allow to stand for 20 minutes. Drain and place the cashews in a blender. Top with the cold water, lemon juice, honey, soy sauce and garlic and blend until smooth. **MAKES 1½ CUPS**

cook's notes

These sauces are true multi-taskers – use them as you would mayonnaise or a creamy salad dressing. The tahini sauce has slightly more tang than the cashew version. The green dressing has a great burst of fresh flavours and will give any dish a real zing – perfect to add to any salad or dish that needs a little lift to finish!

These dressings will keep in a sealed container in the refrigerator for up to 10 days.

smashed hummus

1 x 400g (14 oz) can chickpeas (garbanzo beans),
  drained and rinsed
2 tablespoons hulled tahini
2 tablespoons lemon juice
2 tablespoons extra virgin olive oil
2 tablespoons water
1 clove garlic, crushed
¼ cup (3g/¼ oz) coriander (cilantro) leaves
extra virgin olive oil, extra, to serve
finely shredded lemon rind, to serve
sea salt and cracked black pepper, to serve

Place half the chickpeas in a medium bowl and mash
with a fork until a rough paste forms. Add the remaining
chickpeas and mix to combine. Add the tahini, lemon
juice, oil, water, garlic and coriander and mix to combine.
  Place in a serving bowl and drizzle with extra oil.
Sprinkle with lemon rind, salt and pepper to serve.
MAKES 1½ CUPS

edamame avo smash

1 cup (140g/5 oz) frozen shelled edamame
  beans, blanched
1 avocado, chopped
1 teaspoon finely grated lemon rind
1½ tablespoons lemon juice
sea salt and cracked black pepper
baby (micro) mint leaves, to serve

Place half the edamame beans and the avocado in
a medium bowl and roughly mash with a fork. Add
the lemon rind and juice, salt and pepper and mix
to combine.
  Place in a serving bowl and top with the remaining
edamame. Sprinkle with pepper and the mint leaves
to serve. **MAKES 1¾ CUPS**

cook's note
These simple variations
on guacamole and hummus
have loads of texture, fresh
bursts of lemony flavour
and lots of extra goodness
thrown in. Serve them as
you would any dip, or as
accompaniments to a meal.

seaweed sprinkle

2 sheets toasted nori
2 tablespoons sesame seeds
1 tablespoon light brown sugar
2 teaspoons soy sauce or coconut aminos

Preheat oven to 160°C (325°F). Line 2 large baking trays with non-stick baking paper.

Using scissors, cut the nori sheets into 2cm-wide (1 in) strips, stack them together and snip them into short, fine strips. Place the nori strips in a medium bowl and add the sesame seeds, sugar and soy sauce. Gently toss to combine.

Spread the mixture evenly over the trays. Bake for 5 minutes or until dry and crisp. Allow to cool completely on the trays.

Place in serving bowls for sprinkling, or keep in an airtight container for up to 5 days. **MAKES ¾ CUP**

honey seed sprinkle

½ cup (80g/2¾ oz) pepitas (pumpkin seeds)
¼ cup (40g/1½ oz) sesame seeds
½ cup (80g/2¾ oz) sunflower seeds
¼ cup (90g/3 oz) honey
½ teaspoon cracked black pepper
sea salt flakes, for sprinkling

Line a large baking tray with non-stick baking paper. Place the pepitas, sesame seeds and sunflower seeds in a non-stick frying pan over medium heat. Cook, stirring, for 5 minutes or until toasted.

Add the honey and pepper and cook, stirring constantly, for 1–2 minutes or until the honey has caramelised and the seeds are coated. Spoon onto the tray and sprinkle with salt.

Allow to set completely before roughly chopping. Place in a serving bowl for sprinkling, or keep in an airtight container for up to 10 days. **MAKES 1½ CUPS**

cook's notes

I initially created the honey seed sprinkle to add to my salads and vegie bowls for extra crunch and a hint of salty-sweetness. I've since discovered how amazing it is with fruit and yoghurt or even crumbled over desserts – very versatile (and mildly addictive).

The seaweed sprinkle gives an Asian-style flavour boost and crispy texture to salads, vegies, soups and grilled fish.

seed and nut bread

¼ cup (50g/1¾ oz) chia seeds
¼ cup (20g/¾ oz) psyllium husks
2 cups (320g/11¼ oz) cooked quinoa
1½ cups (375ml/12½ fl oz) water
1 cup (160g/5½ oz) sunflower seeds
½ cup (80g/2¾ oz) flaxseeds (linseeds)
¾ cup (120g/4¼ oz) roughly chopped almonds
¼ cup (60ml/2 fl oz) extra virgin olive oil
2 tablespoons maple syrup
½ teaspoon sea salt flakes

Preheat oven to 160°C (325°F). Line a 10cm x 21cm (4 in x 8 in) loaf tin with non-stick baking paper.

Place the chia seeds, psyllium husks, quinoa and water in a large bowl and mix to combine. Allow to stand for 15 minutes.

Add the sunflower seeds, linseeds, almonds, oil, maple syrup and salt and mix well to combine. Pour the mixture into the tin.

Bake for 1 hour 30 minutes or until firm to the touch. Allow to cool in the tin before turning out and slicing to serve. **MAKES 1 LOAF**

cook's notes

This is bread, but not as we know it! Gluten free and literally packed with good things, it's a great way to get your daily dose of seeds and nuts. Top generously with avocado or nut butter, or serve slices with soup.

Store this loaf in the fridge for up to 5 days. You can also slice and freeze it for whenever you need.

lemon and ginger switchel

60g (2 oz) ginger, thinly sliced
1 lemon, thinly sliced
1.5 litres (50 fl oz) water
¼ cup (60ml/2 fl oz) unfiltered apple cider vinegar
   (see *cook's notes*)
2–3 tablespoons maple syrup or honey

Place the ginger, lemon and water in a large saucepan over low heat for 10 minutes. Remove from the heat, allow to cool slightly and refrigerate until cold.

Pour into a non-reactive (glass, ceramic or plastic) jug and add the vinegar. Stir to combine and add the maple syrup to taste. Keep the switchel, refrigerated, for up to 5 days. **SERVES 6-8**

cucumber and mint green tea

1 cucumber, chopped
¼ cup (4g/¼ oz) mint leaves
⅓ cup (80ml/2¾ fl oz) lemon juice
1.5 litres (50 fl oz) freshly brewed green tea,
   chilled (see *cook's notes*)
2 tablespoons honey
sliced baby cucumbers, extra, to serve
mint leaves, extra, to serve

Place the cucumber, mint and lemon juice in a blender and blend until smooth. Press the mixture through a sieve into a large jug, discarding any solids. Add the tea, stir to combine and add the honey to taste.

Pour the tea over ice into serving glasses and add extra cucumber and mint leaves to serve. Keep the tea, refrigerated, for up to 2 days. **SERVES 4**

cook's notes

You can buy unfiltered or organic apple cider vinegar at supermarkets. Choose bottles labelled as being 'with the mother', which contain original enzymes and good bacteria.

The lemon and ginger switchel is really alkalising. I usually drink mine in the morning, but then I'll find myself sipping on it in the afternoon too! It's very refreshing and a little goes a long way.

I used 2 tablespoons of loose-leafed tea to make the 1.5 litres (50 fl oz) needed for the cucumber and mint green tea recipe.

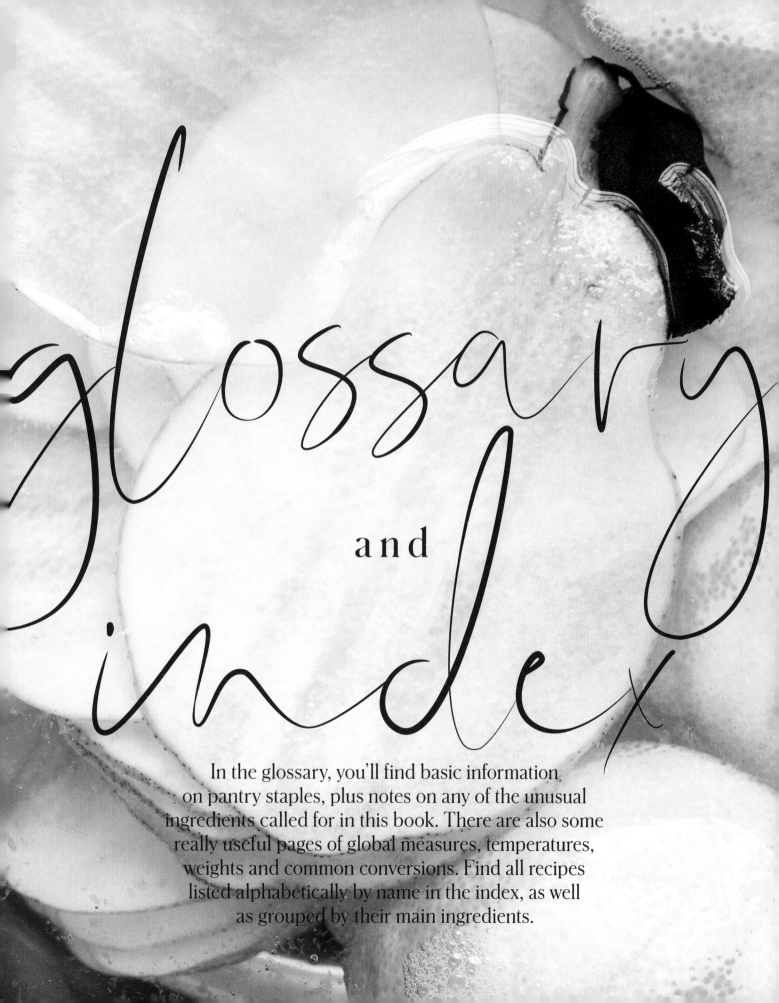

glossary and index

In the glossary, you'll find basic information
on pantry staples, plus notes on any of the unusual
ingredients called for in this book. There are also some
really useful pages of global measures, temperatures,
weights and common conversions. Find all recipes
listed alphabetically by name in the index, as well
as grouped by their main ingredients.

almond butter

This paste is made from ground almonds and is available at most supermarkets and health food stores. It's a popular alternative to peanut butter for those with peanut allergies (always check the label). Sometimes sold as 'spreads', the nut butters called for in this book are all-natural with no additives.

almond meal (ground almonds)

Almond meal is available from most supermarkets. Take care not to confuse it with almond flour, which has a much finer texture. Make your own almond meal by processing whole almonds to a meal in a food processor – 125g (4½ oz) almonds should give 1 cup of almond meal.

barley, pearl

In making pearl barley, the barley husk and bran are removed and the grains are steamed and polished until smooth. When cooked, it's creamy and satisfying in soups, stews and wintry salads. 1 cup cooked pearl barley weighs 185g (6½ oz). Directions for cooking pearl barley are as follows.

1 cup (210g/7½ oz) pearl barley
1¼ cups (310ml/10½ fl oz) water
sea salt flakes

Place the barley, water and a pinch of salt in a medium saucepan over high heat. Bring to the boil, immediately cover with a tight-fitting lid and reduce the heat to low. Simmer for 18 minutes or until almost tender. Remove from the heat and allow to steam for 10 minutes or until tender.
MAKES 2 CUPS (370G/13 OZ)

baking powder

A raising agent used in baking, consisting of bicarbonate of soda and/or cream of tartar. Most are gluten free (check the label). Baking powder that's kept beyond its use-by date can lose effectiveness.

bicarbonate of (baking) soda

Also known as baking soda, bicarbonate of soda (sodium bicarbonate) is an alkaline powder used to help leaven baked goods and neutralise acids.

blanching

Blanching is a cooking method used to slightly soften the texture, heighten the colour and enhance the flavour of foods, namely vegetables. Plunge the ingredient briefly into boiling unsalted water, remove and refresh under cold water. Drain well.

bok choy

Bok choy is a mild-flavoured green vegetable, with fresh crunchy white stems and broad floppy green leaves. It's also known as Chinese chard, Chinese white cabbage or pak choy. It's best trimmed, gently steamed, pan-fried or blanched, then teamed with Asian-style rice dishes or stir-fries.

broccolini (sprouting broccoli)

Also known as tenderstem broccoli, broccolini is a cross between gai lan (Chinese broccoli) and broccoli. This popular green vegetable has long, thin stems and small florets with a slightly sweet flavour. Sold in bunches, it can be substituted with regular heads of broccoli that have been sliced into slim florets.

burghul

Burghul, or bulgur wheat, is wheat kernels that have been steamed, dried and crushed. Used notably in tabouli, find coarse burghul in most supermarkets. 1 cup cooked coarse burghul weighs 165g (5¾ oz). Directions for cooking burghul are as follows.

1 cup (200g/7 oz) coarse burghul

Place the burghul in a large saucepan of salted boiling water over high heat. Reduce the heat to low and simmer, stirring occasionally, for 18 minutes or until tender. Drain well.
MAKES 3⅔ CUPS (600G/1 LB 5 OZ)

butter

Unless it says otherwise in a recipe, butter should be at room temperature for cooking. It should not be half-melted or too soft to handle. We mostly prefer unsalted butter, but use salted if you wish.

buttermilk

Once a by-product of the butter churning process, buttermilk is now created by adding a bacteria to skimmed milk. Its acidity and tangy creaminess is often harnessed to make fluffy pancakes and dressings. It's sold in cartons at supermarkets. A makeshift buttermilk can be made by mixing 1 tablespoon lemon juice into 1 cup (250ml/8½ fl oz) milk. Allow to stand for 5 minutes at room temperature or until just curdled.

cavolo nero (tuscan kale)

Translated to mean 'black cabbage', this dark leafy vegetable is similar to silverbeet, and is super nutritious.

cabbage

chinese

Also known as wombok or Napa cabbage, Chinese cabbage is elongated in shape with ribbed green-yellow leaves. It's regularly used in noodle salads and to make kimchi. Find it at Asian grocers and greengrocers.

green

Pale green or white with tightly bound, waxy leaves, these common cabbages are sold whole or halved in supermarkets and are perfect for use in slaws and sides. Choose heads that are firm and unblemished with crispy leaves that are tightly packed.

capers

These small green flower buds of the caper bush are available packed either in brine or salt. Capers lend their signature salty-sour intensity to sauces, seafood, pastas and more. Before using, rinse thoroughly, drain and pat dry.

cheese

bocconcini

Bite-sized balls of the white fresh mild Italian cheese, mozzarella. Sold in tubs in a lightly salted brine, bocconcini spoils easily so is best consumed within 2–3 days.

buffalo mozzarella

This much-loved variety of fresh Italian mozzarella is made from water buffalo's milk and/or cow's milk. Creamy and salty, it's sold in rounds, or balls, at grocers and delicatessens and is often torn into pieces and scattered over caprese salads or pizza.

burrata

An Italian stretched-curd cheese made from mozzarella, burrata has a creamy, milky centre. It's best served simply, with something like a tomato or fig salad. It's available from delicatessens, specialty cheese stores and Italian grocery stores.

goat's cheese

Goat's milk has a tart flavour, so the cheese made from it, also called chèvre, has a sharp, slightly acidic taste. Immature goat's cheese is mild and creamy and is often labelled goat's curd, which is spreadable. Mature goat's cheese is available in both hard and soft varieties.

haloumi

A firm white Cypriot cheese made from sheep's milk, haloumi has a stringy texture and is usually sold in brine. Slice and pan-fry until golden and heated through for a creamy, salty addition to vegies or salads. Buy haloumi at major greengrocers and supermarkets.

marinated feta

Creamy, mild-tasting Greek-style feta has been marinated in oil, often with a mix of herbs, garlic and peppercorns, to make this cheese.

parmesan

Italy's favourite hard, granular cheese is made from cow's milk. Parmigiano Reggiano is the best variety, made under strict guidelines in the Emilia-Romagna region and aged for an average of two years. Grana Padano mainly comes from Lombardy and is aged for around 15 months.

ricotta

A creamy, finely grained white cheese. Ricotta means 'recooked' in Italian, a reference to the way the cheese is produced by heating the whey leftover from making other cheese varieties. It's fresh, creamy and low in fat and there is also a reduced-fat version, which is lighter again. Choose fresh ricotta from your delicatessen or supermarket deli. Steer away from pre-packaged tubs that are labelled smooth.

chia seeds

These ancient seeds come from a flowering plant and are full of protein, omega-3 fatty acids, minerals and fibre. Use the black or white seeds interchangeably. Find them in supermarkets – they're great for smoothies, salads and baking.

chickpeas (garbanzo beans)

A legume native to western Asia and across the Mediterranean, chickpeas are used in soups, stews and are the base ingredient in hummus. Dried chickpeas need soaking before use; buy them canned to skip this step.

chillies

There are more than 200 different types of chillies, or chilli peppers, in the world. Long red or green chillies are generally milder, fruitier and sweeter, while small chillies are much hotter. Remove the membranes and seeds for a milder result.

chipotle in adobo sauce

Chipotle are smoke-dried jalapeño chillies. In adobo sauce, they're sold in cans or jars at supermarkets, specialty grocers and delicatessens.

jalapeños

These dark green plump Mexican chillies are known for their medium heat and fresh, bitey flavour. Buy jalapeños sliced in jars, pickled or fresh. Often served with tacos and other popular Mexican cuisine, much of their heat is held in the seeds and membranes, which can be removed for a milder intensity.

chinese cooking wine (shaoxing)

Similar to dry sherry, Shaoxing, or Chinese cooking wine, is a blend of glutinous rice, millet, a special yeast and the local spring waters of Shaoxing in northern China, where it is traditionally made. Used in myriad sauces and dressings, it's available from the Asian section of supermarkets and at Asian grocery stores.

chinese five-spice powder

A fragrant ground blend of cinnamon, Sichuan pepper, star anise, cloves and fennel seeds, five spice is a popular seasoning for duck and pork. It also goes well with chicken and vegetables. It's an essential ingredient in slow-braised Chinese dishes. Available at Asian food stores, spice shops and supermarkets.

chocolate

dark

Rich and semi-sweet, regular dark chocolate usually contains 45–55% cocoa solids. It's sold in blocks and is ideal for use in baking. Dark chocolate that has 70% cocoa solids is usually labelled as such, and has a more bitter, intense flavour with a slightly powdery texture.

milk

Sweet, creamy and smooth, with a lighter colour than dark chocolate, milk chocolate is the most popular for eating. Sold in blocks, it usually contains around 25% cocoa solids.

coconut

aminos

An increasingly popular alternative to soy sauce and fish sauce, coconut aminos is made out of sap collected from coconut blossoms, which is combined with sea salt and naturally aged. Find it in major greengrocers, some supermarkets and at health food stores. It's generally both soy and gluten free, but check the label.

cream

The cream that rises to the top after the first pressing of coconut milk, coconut cream is higher both in energy and fat than regular coconut milk. A common ingredient in curries and Asian sweets, you can buy it in cans or cartons from the supermarket.

desiccated

Desiccated coconut is coconut meat that has been shredded and dried to remove its moisture. It's unsweetened and very powdery. Great for baking as well as savoury Asian sauces and sambals.

flakes

Coconut flakes have a large shape and chewier texture than the desiccated variety, and are often used for decorating and in cereals and baking. You can buy coconut flakes ready-toasted, with lovely golden edges, from supermarkets.

milk

A milky, sweet liquid made by soaking grated fresh coconut flesh or desiccated coconut in warm water and squeezing it through muslin or cheesecloth. Available in cartons or cans or from the supermarket, coconut milk should not be confused with coconut water, which is a clear liquid found inside young coconuts. The recipes in this book have been made using coconut milk from cartons, as it tends to be superior in quality and flavour.

oil

Extracted from mature coconuts, coconut oil is sold in jars as a solid, so you may need to melt it before using. It adds a touch of tropical flavour to baked treats and slices and is often used as a dairy-free alternative to butter. Look for virgin coconut oil in supermarkets and health food stores.

shredded

In slightly larger pieces than desiccated, shredded coconut is great for adding a bit more texture to slices and cakes, or for making condiments to serve with curries.

sugar

See *sugar (coconut)*, page 248.

yoghurt

Coconut yoghurt has become far more readily available in recent years, thanks to its dairy-free status. It's made from coconut milk and probiotic cultures. Find it in the chilled yoghurt section of most supermarkets and in specialty grocers and health food stores.

coriander (cilantro)

This pungent green herb is common in Asian and Mexican cooking. The finely chopped roots are sometimes incorporated into curry pastes. The dried seeds can't be substituted for fresh coriander.

dukkah

A Middle-Eastern nut and spice blend available from some supermarkets, from spice shops and specialty grocery stores. Great for sprinkling on meats and salads or using in a spice crust.

edamame

Find these tasty, tender soy beans ready-podded in the freezer section of major greengrocers, Asian grocers and some supermarkets.

eggs

The standard egg size used in this book is 60g (2 oz). It's important to use the right sized eggs, for baking recipes especially, as it can affect the outcome. Room temperature eggs are best for baking.

fish sauce

This amber-coloured liquid drained from salted, fermented fish and is used to add flavour to Thai and Vietnamese dishes, such as curries, plus dressings and dipping sauces.

flaxseeds (linseeds)

These small brown seeds have a nutty flavour and are high in omega-3. They can be baked into bread, sprinkled in cereal and salads or used to make slices. Find them at supermarkets and health food stores.

flour

buckwheat

Despite its name, buckwheat flour isn't from a grain but is milled from the seed of a plant related to rhubarb and sorrel. Often used in pancakes and noodles for its rich, nutty flavour and wholesome benefits, it's also gluten free.

cornflour (cornstarch)

When made from ground corn or maize, cornflour is gluten free. Recipes often require it to be blended with water or stock for a thickening agent. Not to be confused with cornflour in the United States, which is finely ground corn meal.

plain (all-purpose)

Ground from the endosperm of wheat, plain white flour contains no raising agent.

rice

Rice flour is a fine flour made from ground rice. Available in white and brown varieties, it's often used as a thickening agent in baking, in cookies and shortbreads, and to coat foods when cooking Asian dishes. It's gluten free and available in supermarkets and health food shops.

self-raising (self-rising)

Ground from the endosperm of wheat, self-raising flour contains raising agents including sodium carbonates and calcium phosphates.

spelt

Milled from the ancient cereal grain, spelt flour boasts more nutrients and is better tolerated by some than regular flour.

wholemeal (whole-wheat)

Ground from the whole grain of wheat and thus keeping more of its nutrients and fibre, this flour is available in plain (all-purpose) and self-raising (self-rising) varieties from most supermarkets and health food stores.

freekeh

Freekeh is the immature or 'green' wheat grain that's been roasted. The recipes in this book call for whole-grain freekeh as opposed to cracked freekeh. The grains can be used in vegetable salads and tabouli or eat it as you would rice or pasta. Find it in supermarkets and health food stores. 1 cup cooked freekeh weighs 160g (5½ oz). Directions for cooking freekeh are as follows.

1 cup (220g/7¾ oz) freekeh
3 cups (750ml/25 fl oz) water

Place the freekeh and water in a medium saucepan over high heat. Bring to the boil, immediately cover with a tight-fitting lid and reduce the heat to low. Cook for 30–35 minutes or until tender. Drain any remaining water. **MAKES 3 CUPS (480G/1 LB)**

gai lan (chinese broccoli)

Also known as Chinese broccoli or Chinese kale, gai lan is a leafy vegetable with dark green leaves, tiny white or yellow flowers and stout stems. It can be steamed or blanched and served with oyster sauce as a simple side or added to soups, stir-fries and braises towards the end of the cooking time. Gai lan is sold in bunches at greengrocers and supermarkets.

gow gee wrappers

Chinese in origin, these round, thin sheets of dough are available chilled or frozen. They can be steamed or fried. Fill them with meat and vegetables to make dumplings, or use as a crunchy base for nibbles.

green onions (scallions)

Both the white and green part of these long mild onions are used in salads, as a garnish and in Asian cooking. Sold in bunches, they give a fresh bite to dishes.

hemp seeds

These mild, nutty-flavoured seeds are of the hemp plant and contain loads of protein, essential fatty acids and fibre. Find them at health food stores.

horseradish

A pungent root vegetable that releases mustard oil when cut or grated, horseradish is available fresh from greengrocers. You can substitute it with pre-grated or creamed varieties sold in jars.

juniper berries

The aromatic and bitter dried berries of a hardy evergreen bush, juniper is used for pickling vegetables and flavouring sauces.

kaffir lime leaves

Fragrant leaves from the kaffir lime tree have a distinctive double-leaf structure. Commonly crushed or shredded and used in Thai dishes, the leaves are available, fresh or dried, from most greengrocers and at Asian food stores. Fresh leaves are more flavourful and freeze well.

labne

Find this creamy Middle-Eastern yoghurt cheese in tubs in the chilled section of greengrocers, gourmet food stores and some supermarkets.

lemongrass

Lemongrass is a tall lemon-scented grass used in Asian cooking, mainly in Thai dishes. Peel away the outer leaves and chop the tender white root-end finely, or add in large pieces during cooking and remove before serving. If adding in larger pieces, bruise them with the back of a kitchen knife.

maple syrup

A sweetener made from the sap of the maple tree, be sure to use pure maple syrup. Imitation, or pancake, syrup is made from corn syrup flavoured with maple and does not have the same intensity of flavour.

mirin (japanese rice wine)

Mirin is a pale yellow, sweet and tangy Japanese cooking wine made from glutinous rice and alcohol.

miso paste

Miso is a traditional Japanese ingredient produced by fermenting rice, barley or soy beans to a paste. It's used for sauces and spreads, pickling vegetables, and is often mixed with dashi stock to serve as miso soup. Sometimes labelled simply 'miso', white, yellow and red varieties are available, their flavour increasing in intensity with their colour. The recipes in this book call on white miso (shiro) for its delicate flavour and colour. Find miso paste in supermarkets and Asian grocers.

nori

Nori sheets are paper-thin layers of dried seaweed, commonly used for making sushi rolls. High in protein and minerals, nori can also be chopped, added to soups or used as a garnish. Buy nori, ready-toasted if necessary, at most supermarkets, at greengrocers and Asian grocers.

paprika, smoked

Unlike Hungarian paprika, the Spanish style, known as pimentón, is deep and smoky in flavour. It is made from smoked, ground pimento peppers and comes in varying intensities, from sweet and mild (dulce), bittersweet medium hot (agridulce) and hot (picante). The variety called for in this book is smoky-sweet.

pastry

Make your own or use one of the many store-bought varieties, including shortcrust and filo, which are sold frozen in blocks or ready-rolled into pastry sheets. Defrost in the fridge before use.

puff and butter puff

This pastry is quite difficult to make, so many cooks opt to use store-bought puff pastry. It can be bought in blocks from patisseries, or sold in both block and sheet forms in supermarkets. Butter puff pastry is very light and flaky, perfect for both savoury and sweet pies and tarts. Often labelled 'all butter puff', good-quality sheets are usually thicker. If you can only buy thin sheets of butter puff, don't be afraid to stack 2 regular thawed sheets together.

pepitas (pumpkin seeds)

Pumpkin seeds are hulled to reveal these olive green kernels that, once dried, are nutty in flavour and easy to use in smoothies, baking and salads. Find them in supermarkets.

pickled ginger

Also known as gari, this Japanese condiment is made from young ginger that's been pickled in sugar and vinegar. It's commonly served with japanese food as a palate cleanser, but is becoming popular as a tangy addition to sushi bowls and salads. Buy it in jars from Asian grocers and some supermarkets.

pomegranate molasses

A concentrated syrup made from pomegranate juice, with a sweet, tart flavour, pomegranate molasses is available from Middle Eastern grocery stores and specialty food shops. If you can't find it, try using caramelised balsamic vinegar.

porcini mushrooms

Available fresh in Europe and the UK and sold dried elsewhere, including Australia and the US, porcini have an almost meaty texture and earthy taste. Soak dried porcini before using, and use the soaking liquid as a stock if desired. Frozen porcini is becoming more readily available. Like the dried variety, it's available from specialty food stores.

psyllium husks

The husks of psyllium seeds are available in health food shops and some supermarkets. Super-rich in fibre, they're used in gluten-free baking as a binding ingredient.

quinoa

Packed with protein, this grain-like seed has a chewy texture, nutty flavour and is fluffy when cooked. Use it as you would couscous or rice. It freezes well, so any excess cooked quinoa can be frozen in individual portions. Red and black varieties, which require a slightly longer cooking time, are also available in most supermarkets. 1 cup cooked white quinoa weighs 160g (5½ oz). Directions for cooking quinoa are as follows.

1 cup (180g/6¼ oz) white quinoa
1¼ cups (310ml/10½ fl oz) water
sea salt flakes

Place the quinoa, water and a pinch of salt in a medium saucepan over high heat. Bring to the boil, cover immediately with a tight-fitting lid and reduce the heat to low. Simmer for 12 minutes or until almost tender. Remove from the heat and allow to steam for 8 minutes or until tender. **MAKES 2¾ CUPS (440G/15½ OZ)**

flakes

Quinoa flakes are simply quinoa seeds that have been steamrolled into flakes. Use them in breakfast cereals or baked goods. Find them in health food shops and supermarkets.

ras el hanout

A North African spice mix, literally translating as 'top of the shop', ras el hanout can contain more than 20 different spices – most commonly cinnamon, cardamom, coriander, cloves, chilli, paprika and turmeric. Find it at spice shops, gourmet grocers and most supermarkets.

raw cacao

powder

Available in nibs and powder form, raw cacao comes from tropical cacao beans that have been cold pressed. Rich, dark and pleasantly bitter; find it in most supermarkets.

chocolate

Cacao chocolate comes in bars or blocks that have been made with raw cacao. It's sold in select grocers and health food shops.

rice, brown

Brown rice is different to white rice in that the bran and germ of the wholegrain are intact. This renders it nutritionally superior and gives it a nutty chewiness. 1 cup cooked brown rice weighs 200g (7 oz). Directions for cooking brown rice are as follows.

1 cup (200g/7 oz) brown rice
1½ cups (375ml/12½ fl oz) water
sea salt flakes

Place the rice, water and a pinch of salt in a medium saucepan over high heat. Bring to the boil, immediately cover with a tight-fitting lid and reduce the heat to low. Simmer for 25 minutes or until almost tender. Remove from the heat and allow to steam for 10 minutes or until tender. **MAKES 2 CUPS (400G/14 OZ)**

rosewater

An essence distilled from rose petals, rosewater is one of the cornerstone flavours of Indian and Middle-Eastern tables. Usually used in sweets, it's the distinctive flavour in Turkish delight (lokum).

sage

This Mediterranean herb has a distinct, fragrant flavour and soft, oval-shaped grey-green leaves. It's used often in Italian cooking, crisped in a pan with butter or oil.

spelt

This ancient cereal grain is part of the wider wheat family. It has a mild, nutty flavour and when cooked it becomes plump and chewy. Add cooked spelt to salads and soups, or use it as a wholesome alternative to rice or pasta. 1 cup cooked spelt weighs 200g (7 oz). Directions for cooking spelt are as follows.

1 cup (200g/7 oz) spelt
1¼ cups (310ml/10½ fl oz) water
sea salt flakes

Place the spelt, water and a pinch of salt in a medium saucepan over high heat. Bring to the boil, immediately cover with a tight-fitting lid and reduce the heat to low. Simmer for 20 minutes or until almost tender. Remove from the heat and allow to steam for 10 minutes or until tender. **MAKES 2 CUPS (400G/14 OZ)**

sesame seeds

These small seeds have a nutty flavour and can be used in savoury and sweet cooking. White sesame seeds are the most common variety, but black, or unhulled, seeds are popular for coatings in Asian cooking.

shichimi togarashi

A common Japanese spice mixture of ground chilli, orange peel, sesame seeds and more, find togarashi at Asian and gourmet grocers.

silverbeet (swiss chard)

A vegetable with large, crinkly, glossy dark green leaves and prominent white, red or yellow stalks, silverbeet is rich in nutrients. It can be used in salads, soups, pies and steamed as a side. Not to be confused with English spinach which has a smaller and more delicate leaf, silverbeet is best trimmed and washed before use.

sriracha hot chilli sauce

A hot sauce containing chilli, salt, sugar, vinegar and garlic, sriracha is both the brand name of a popular American blend, as well as the generic name for the Southeast-Asian sauce. Use sriracha as a condiment or in marinades. Find it in supermarkets.

sugar

Extracted as crystals from the juice of the sugar cane plant, sugar is a sweetener, flavour enhancer and food preservative.

brown

In Australia, what is known as 'brown sugar' is referred to as 'light brown sugar' in other parts of the world. Light and dark brown sugars are made from refined sugar with natural molasses added. The amount, or percentage, of molasses in relation to the sugar determines its classification as dark or light. The molasses gives the sugar a smooth caramel flavour and also a soft, slightly moist texture. Light and dark types are interchangeable if either is unavailable. An important ingredient in cookies, puddings, dense cakes and brownies, you can find both varieties of brown sugar in supermarkets.

caster (superfine)

The superfine granule of caster sugar gives baked products a light texture and crumb, which is important for many cakes and delicate desserts. Caster sugar is essential for making meringue, as the fine crystals dissolve more easily in the whipped eggwhite.

coconut

With an earthy, butterscotch taste, coconut sugar, or coconut palm sugar, comes from the flowers of the coconut palm. It gives a lovely depth of flavour. Find it in some supermarkets, specialty food shops, Asian grocers and health food stores.

demerara

Demerara is a coarse-grained golden cane sugar, with a mild molasses flavour. Like raw sugar, it's delicious stirred into coffee or sprinkled over baked treats for a sweet caramel crust.

icing (confectioner's)

Regular granulated sugar ground to a very fine powder. It often clumps together and needs to be sifted before using. Unless specified in a recipe, use pure icing sugar not icing sugar mixture, which contains cornflour (cornstarch).

palm

Produced by tapping the sap of palm trees, palm sugar is allowed to crystallise and is sold in cubes or round blocks, which you can shave and add to curries, dressings and Asian desserts. Available from some supermarkets and Asian food stores.

rapadura
Extracted from the pure juice of cane sugar, rapadura (or panela) is evaporated over low heat, which means some minerals and vitamins in the cane are retained. Find this sugar at major supermarkets and health food stores.

raw
Light brown in colour and honey-like in flavour, raw sugar is slightly less refined than white sugar, with a larger granule. It lends a more pronounced flavour and colour to baked goods. You can use demerara sugar in its place.

white (granulated)
Regular granulated sugar is used in baking when a light texture is not crucial. The crystals are larger, so you need to beat, add liquids or heat this sugar if you want to dissolve it.

sumac
These dried berries of a flowering plant are ground to produce an acidic, vibrant crimson powder that's popular in the Middle East. Sumac has a lemony flavour and is great sprinkled on salads, dips or chicken. Find it at specialty spice shops, greengrocers and some supermarkets.

sunflower seeds
These small grey kernels from the black and white seeds of sunflowers are mostly processed for their oil. The kernels are also found in snack mixes and muesli, and can be baked into breads and slices. Buy sunflower seeds in supermarkets and health food stores.

tahini
A thick paste made from ground sesame seeds, tahini is widely used in Middle-Eastern cooking. It's available in jars and cans from supermarkets and health food shops, in both hulled and unhulled varieties. The recipes in this book call for hulled tahini, for its slightly smoother texture.

tofu
Not all tofu is created equal. The recipes in this book call for either firm or silken tofu, which can be found in the chilled section of the supermarket. Where possible, choose an organic non-GMO option and remember that all brands vary in texture and taste. Don't give up until you find one you love. It's inexpensive, a great source of protein and acts like a sponge for flavour.

vanilla
bean paste
This store-bought paste is a convenient way to replace whole vanilla beans and is great in desserts. One teaspoon of paste substitutes for one vanilla bean.

beans
These fragrant cured pods from the vanilla orchid are used whole, often split with the tiny seeds inside scraped into the mixture to infuse flavour into custard and cream-based recipes. They offer a rich and rounded vanilla flavour.

extract
For a pure vanilla taste, use a good-quality vanilla extract, not an essence or imitation flavour.

vinegar
apple cider
Made from apple must, cider vinegar has a golden amber hue and a sour appley flavour. Use it in dressings, marinades and chutneys. The recipes in this book call for organic or unfiltered apple cider vinegar.

balsamic
Originally from Modena in Italy, there are many balsamics on the market ranging in quality and flavour. Aged varieties are generally preferable. A milder white version is also available, which is used in dishes where the colour is important.

rice wine
Made from fermenting rice (or rice wine), rice vinegar is milder and sweeter than vinegars that are made by oxidising distilled wine or other alcohol made from grapes. Rice wine vinegar is available in white (colourless to pale yellow), black, brown and red varieties from Asian food stores and supermarkets.

wasabi paste
We know this Japanese paste for its powdery green colour and its heat. Similar to (and most-likely containing) horseradish, wasabi paste is used as an ingredient and popular condiment for sushi. It's sold, usually in tubes, at Asian grocers and supermarkets.

yoghurt, natural Greek-style
Recipes in this book call for natural, unsweetened full-fat Greek-style (thick) yoghurt. Buy it from the chilled aisle of the supermarket, checking the label for any unwanted sweeteners or artificial flavours.

global measures

Measures vary from Europe to the US and even from Australia to New Zealand.

liquids and solids

Measuring cups, spoons and scales are great assets in the kitchen – these equivalents are just a general guide.

more equivalents

Here are a few more simplified equivalents for metric and imperial measures, plus ingredient names.

metric and imperial

Measuring cups and spoons may vary slightly from one country to another, but the difference is generally not sufficient to affect a recipe. The recipes in this book use Australian measures (with American conversions). All cup and spoon measures are level. An Australian measuring cup holds 250ml (8½ fl oz).

One Australian metric teaspoon holds 5ml (⅛ fl oz), one Australian tablespoon holds 20ml (¾ fl oz) (4 teaspoons). However, in the USA, New Zealand and the UK, 15ml (½ fl oz) (3-teaspoon) tablespoons are used.

If measuring liquid ingredients, remember that 1 American pint contains 475ml (16 fl oz) but 1 imperial pint contains 570ml (19 fl oz).

When measuring dry ingredients, add the ingredient loosely to the cup and level with a knife. Don't tap or shake to compact the ingredient unless the recipe requests 'firmly packed'.

liquids

cup	metric	imperial
⅛ cup	30ml	1 fl oz
¼ cup	60ml	2 fl oz
⅓ cup	80ml	2¾ fl oz
½ cup	125ml	4¼ fl oz
⅔ cup	160ml	5½ fl oz
¾ cup	180ml	6 fl oz
1 cup	250ml	8½ fl oz
2 cups	500ml	17 fl oz
3 cups	750ml	25 fl oz
4 cups	1 litre	34 fl oz

solids

metric	imperial
20g	¾ oz
60g	2 oz
125g	4½ oz
180g	6¼ oz
250g	8¾ oz
450g	1 lb
750g	1 lb 10 oz
1kg	2 lb 3 oz

millimetres to inches

metric	imperial
3mm	⅛ inch
6mm	¼ inch
1cm	½ inch
2.5cm	1 inch
5cm	2 inches
18cm	7 inches
20cm	8 inches
23cm	9 inches
25cm	10 inches
30cm	12 inches

ingredient equivalents

almond meal	ground almonds
bicarbonate of soda	baking soda
caster sugar	superfine sugar
celeriac	celery root
chickpeas	garbanzo beans
coriander	cilantro
cornflour	cornstarch
cos lettuce	romaine lettuce
eggplant	aubergine
gai lan	chinese broccoli
green onion	scallion
icing sugar	confectioner's sugar
plain flour	all-purpose flour
rocket	arugula
self-raising flour	self-rising flour
silverbeet	swiss chard
snow pea	mange tout
white sugar	granulated sugar
zucchini	courgette

oven temperatures

Setting the oven to the correct temperature can be crucial when baking sweet things.

celsius to fahrenheit

celsius	fahrenheit
100°C	200°F
120°C	250°F
140°C	275°F
150°C	300°F
160°C	325°F
180°C	350°F
190°C	375°F
200°C	400°F
220°C	425°F

electric to gas

celsius	gas
110°C	¼
130°C	½
140°C	1
150°C	2
170°C	3
180°C	4
190°C	5
200°C	6
220°C	7
230°C	8
240°C	9
250°C	10

butter and eggs

Let 'fresh is best' be your mantra when it comes to selecting eggs and dairy goods.

butter

We generally use unsalted butter as it allows for a little more control over a recipe's flavour. Either way, the impact is minimal. Salted butter has a longer shelf life and is preferred by some people. One American stick of butter is 125g (4½ oz). One Australian block of butter is 250g (8¾ oz).

eggs

Unless otherwise indicated, we use large (60g/2 oz) chicken eggs. To preserve freshness, store eggs in the refrigerator in the carton they are sold in. Use only the freshest eggs in recipes such as mayonnaise or dressings that use raw or barely cooked eggs. Be extra cautious if there is a salmonella problem in your community, particularly in food that is to be served to children, pregnant women or the elderly.

useful weights

Here are a few simple weight conversions for cupfuls of commonly used ingredients.

common ingredients

almond meal (ground almonds)
1 cup | 120g | 4¼ oz
brown sugar
1 cup | 175g | 6 oz
white (granulated) sugar
1 cup | 220g | 7¾ oz
caster (superfine) sugar
1 cup | 220g | 7¾ oz
icing (confectioner's) sugar
1 cup | 160g | 5½ oz
**plain (all-purpose)
or self-raising (self-rising) flour**
1 cup | 150g | 5¼ oz
fresh breadcrumbs
1 cup | 70g | 2½ oz
finely grated parmesan
1 cup | 80g | 2¾ oz
uncooked white rice
1 cup | 200g | 7 oz
cooked white rice
1 cup | 165g | 5¾ oz
uncooked couscous
1 cup | 200g | 7 oz
**cooked shredded chicken,
pork or beef**
1 cup | 160g | 5½ oz
olives
1 cup | 150g | 5¼ oz

a

almond meal, how to make 240

apple
and raspberry granola slice 190
salad, warm 106

arugula – *see* rocket

avocado
black bean and tomato
tacos 156
edamame avo smash 230

b

banh mi, tofu 16

beef
char-grilled steak and mushroom
open sandwiches 40
thai salad 34

beet and freekeh salad,
roasted 90

beetroot – *see* beet

best vegie burgers 20

biscuits – *see* cookies; slice

blueberry granola cookies 188

bread, seed and nut 234

broccoli
balls, miso brown rice 96
charred roasted, and
haloumi 110
dough 146
flatbread salad sandwiches 150
margherita pizzas 148
pasta with lemon cashew-cream
sauce 58
pesto 38
pumpkin, sage and goat's
cheese tart 152
salad, char-grilled 92

brown rice, how to cook 245

brussels sprouts – *see* sprouts

burgers, best vegie 20

buttermilk
chicken, crispy, with sprout
and celeriac slaw 36
how to make 240
slaw 18

c

cabbage
buttermilk slaw 18
charred, and warm apple
salad 106
miso japanese pancakes 100

caesar salad, chicken, with
crispy kale 26

cake, lemon thyme, honey
and almond 196

carrot
cake and cashew bites, raw 220
miso salad 96
and pickled ginger salad 100
roasted, and turmeric soup 80

cashew
creamy sauce 228
raw carrot cake bites 220

cauliflower
chipotle chicken tacos 24
-rice bowls, spicy peanut 64

celeriac and sprout slaw 36

celery root – *see* celeriac

chard rolls 98

char-grilled fennel, freekeh and
labne salad 76

char-grilled steak and mushroom
open sandwiches 40

charred cabbage and warm
apple salad 106

charred roasted broccoli
and haloumi 110

cheat's chilli cashew tofu larb 52

cheesecake, lemon and
yoghurt 200

chicken
caesar salad with crispy kale 26
chipotle chicken and cauliflower
tacos 24
crispy buttermilk, with sprout
and celeriac slaw 36
crunchy quinoa schnitzels with
buttermilk slaw 18

chilli, lime and ginger thai
tofu cakes 22

chipotle chicken and cauliflower
tacos 24

choc-chunk cookies
ice-cream sandwiches 180
share 176
tahini 174

choc-fudge popsicles 198

chocolate
chunk cookie ice-cream
sandwiches 180
chunk share cookies 176
chunk tahini cookies 174
drizzle cookies, coconut and
sour cherry 178
fudge popsicles 198
and miso caramel slice 204
and raspberry cupcakes 208

cinnamon almond cookies 206

coconut
cucumber-noodle bowls with
crispy fish 62
dressing 62
lemon curd 200
and passionfruit crème brûlée 212
pineapple sherbet 218
and sour cherry chocolate
drizzle cookies 178
wafers 216

cookies
blueberry granola 188
choc-chunk, ice-cream
sandwiches 180
choc-chunk tahini 174
cinnamon almond 206
coconut and sour cherry
chocolate drizzle 178
double choc-chunk share 174
raw caramel oat 214

courgette – *see* zucchini

creamy cashew sauce 228

crème brûlée, passionfruit
and coconut 212

crispy buttermilk chicken with
sprout and celeriac slaw 36

crispy chia salmon 94

This is the first book I've created in my new studio. It's such an inspiring space, but building a bespoke filming and test kitchen a few weeks before we started shooting meant it was all hands on deck for a little while. The people I had around me have, without question, made this book possible.

To the dh dream team, Virginia Ford, Ruby Gillard, Hannah Schubert and Claudia De Berardinis, it's not lost on me that you all have my back, in the office, on the daily. You use your expertise (and humour) to support me in every way that you can. I'm forever grateful.

Con Poulos, even in the earliest stages, I knew that this book required your special touch. We've known each other for a very long time and I needed your calm, considered nature around me in the studio. Thank you, not just for these stunning images, but for your friendship – I treasure it.

To my trusted creative director, Chi Lam, it's been so many years now, but you never fail to wow me with what you (seemingly!) effortlessly create. Your ideas are endless and you have a magical talent for taking my books to the next level.

Abby Pfahl, my editor, thank you for weaving my vision onto these pages in your perfect words. I'm so grateful for your insight and discernment.

I'm very lucky to have you in my in-house design team, Hannah Schubert. Your attention to detail, fabulous creativity and work ethic make you a total triple-threat, plus you're so lovely to be around!

Helping me with merchandising for this project (plus everything that comes along with that) were Alex and Andreas Zehntner. Nothing's a problem for these two, they're the yin and yang of creative, which is exactly what I need in a styling team.

Tessa Immens, I really appreciate your reliable, careful talent in the kitchen – it's a must for both testing and for photography. Madeleine Jeffreys, you're my queen of all the important details and it was so fun to work with you. Samantha Coutts, thanks for always bringing such a good attitude and your great skills – it's always a pleasure.

At HarperCollins*Publishers*, I absolutely need to thank James Kellow, Catherine Milne, Janelle Garside and Belinda Yuille for their ongoing dedication and faith in me.

Thank you to my loyal brand partners – CSR Sugar, Smeg, Cobram Estate, Le Creuset, Estée Lauder, KitchenAid and Cloudy Bay – I'm so proud to work with you all. I'd also like to thank MCM House, Zip Water, Smartstone, Lee Matthews, The Beach People and Broadleaf Joinery – all of whom have contributed their amazing creations to this book.

Wormticklers Nursery, Kurrawong Organics, Sift Produce, Murdoch Produce and Martin's Seafood – I love working with your beautiful businesses, thanks for your exceptional harvests and for being so generous with your knowledge.

I was lucky enough to collaborate with some local artists and ceramicists for this book. Most of them dropped into the studio at some point for a chat (and a cookie!) – such a spirited group of happy creatives. You'll see their lovely wares throughout these pages.
Splendid Wren Ceramics @splendidwrenceramics
Little White Dish @littlewhitedish
The Potter x The Clay @thepotterxtheclay
Hayden Youlley @haydenyoulley
Shut Up and Relax @shutupandrelax
Sarah Jerath @sarahjerath

Last but not least, I'm sending big thank yous to my friends and family – you give me all the flexibility and love a girl could wish for. Karen Hay, your early morning advice on all things (especially financial) means the world. An extra mention this year must go to my boys (big and small), who actually appear in the book with me – we had so many laughs on location – you're my new favourite models!

about donna

Snoop through any self-respecting Australian's cookbook collection, and you'll find something by Donna Hay. As Australia's leading food editor and bestselling cookbook author, she's made her way into hearts (and nearly every home) across the country.

An international publishing phenomenon, Donna Hay's name is synonymous with a style of new-world cuisine that looks chic and modern, is quick and easy to prepare for the home cook but has an emphasis on real flavour. Her highly acclaimed bi-monthly food title, *donna hay magazine*, notched up an incredible 100 issues – a milestone number – before she ceased publishing it in 2018.

The magazine made Donna a household name, reaching subscribers in 82 countries around the world. But the donna hay brand encompasses more than that – over the past 20 years, she has written 29 bestselling cookbooks, with more than seven million copies sold worldwide, and hosted TV series screened in at least 17 countries. Donna has her own homewares range and an expanding collection of baking mixes available at supermarkets around Australia. She is the very proud mum of two teenage boys, adores living near the ocean and is newly obsessed with her little organic vegetable garden.